AF521810

Reimagining History from an Indigenous Perspective

The Graphic Work of Floyd Solomon

REIMAGINING HISTORY FROM AN INDIGENOUS PERSPECTIVE

Joyce M. Szabo

Introduction by Siegfried Halus

UNIVERSITY OF NEW MEXICO PRESS | ALBUQUERQUE

Printed in the United States of America

ISBN 978-0-8263-6409-8 (paper)
ISBN 978-0-8263-6410-4 (electronic)

Library of Congress Control Number: 2022940014

Founded in 1889, the University of New Mexico sits on the traditional homelands of the Pueblo of Sandia. The original peoples of New Mexico—Pueblo, Navajo, and Apache—since time immemorial have deep connections to the land and have made significant contributions to the broader community statewide. We honor the land itself and those who remain stewards of this land throughout the generations and also acknowledge our committed relationship to Indigenous peoples. We gratefully recognize our history.

Cover photograph: © Siegfried Halus, courtesy of Maximilian Halus
Designed by Felicia Cedillos
Composed in Utopia Std 10.5/15.4

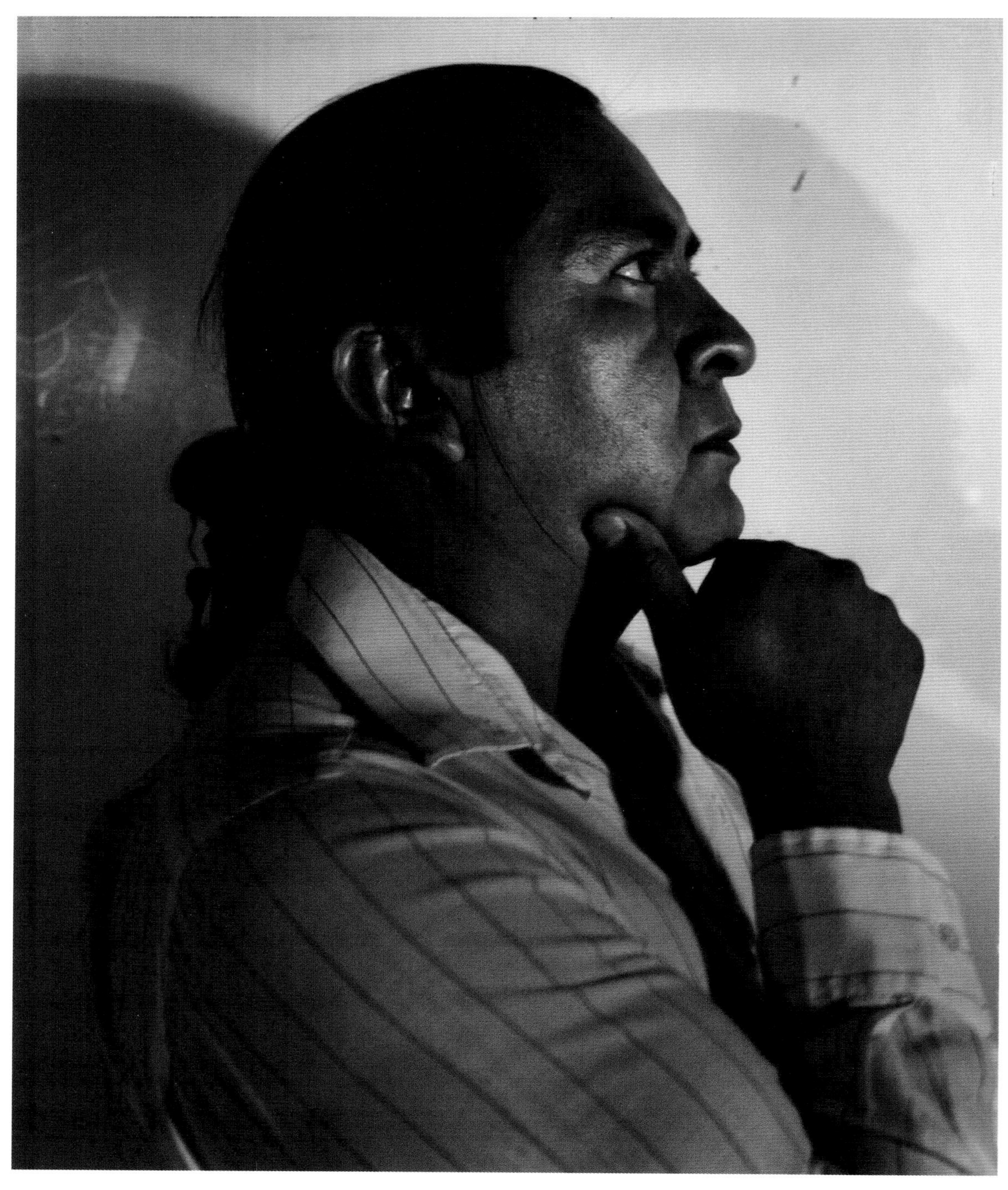

Figure 1. Siegfried Halus, *Floyd Solomon*, 1994. Gelatin silver print, 15 ⅜ × 12 ⅝ in.

CONTENTS

PREFACE

Siegfried Halus (1943–2018) and I began the journey together that led to this book more than seven years ago. We cocurated an exhibition of Floyd Solomon's work at the University of New Mexico Museum of Art in Spring 2014, and, following the end of that show, we both agreed that the artist deserved far more attention. We each began working on our parts of what follows.

While I had only met Floyd a couple of times, Siegfried knew him well. Thus it made perfect sense for Siegfried to write the introduction, almost a dedication, for the work. My parts are more academically focused.

Both Siegfried and I decided that we would not seek publication of this manuscript if officials at Laguna did not approve of it. Subsequently we met with the governor and several tribal members who had previously read the manuscript. They approved our publication of it provided we included the disclaimer that follows this preface; we readily agreed.

Unfortunately, Siegfried unexpectedly passed away before the book could be published. To the end of his life he was dedicated to pursuing the goal we began together and would have been extremely gratified to see that our ends have finally been achieved.

I also acknowledge the encouragement that the late Lisa Tamaris Becker (d. 2016), then director of the University of New Mexico Art Museum, and the entire museum staff offered to Siegfried and me for our exhibition of Floyd's work. Margot Geist, of Geistlight Photography, brought her great sensitivity to her photography of Floyd's work and to this project.

This book and the previous exhibition would not have been possible without the support and enthusiasm of Jeanne Solomon Bell. She knew Siegfried well and also spoke with me multiple times about Floyd. She lent the majority of her husband's work that appeared in the exhibition and that is included in this volume. Of particular value to me were Floyd's sketchbooks, which provide not only preliminary drawings and ideas for completed etchings but also notes to himself about what he could adjust in various prints. Other brief handwritten passages relate to the events he was portraying and the emotions he was trying to relay. These were pivotal to the label copy for the exhibition. The most important and sincere compliment that I overheard at the show's opening was from one of Floyd's sisters, who said that the labels sounded as if Floyd were speaking. I have followed the same approach here that I did in the exhibition text.

DISCLAIMER

The events, beliefs, and opinions depicted in this document are based on personal interviews the author(s) have had with Floyd Solomon and Solomon's own writings and recorded statements. These events and beliefs do not depict any actual events at the Pueblo of Laguna as handed down through oral history by the Pueblo's forefathers. The writings contained in this document are the authors' interpretations of Mr. Solomon's illustrated expressions of his personal feelings about events that occurred during the course of Pueblo history. None of these events, beliefs, or opinions expressed by the authors are those of the Pueblo of Laguna.

Gaylord Siow
Tribal Historic Preservation Officer
Pueblo of Laguna

REIMAGINING HISTORY FROM
AN INDIGENOUS PERSPECTIVE

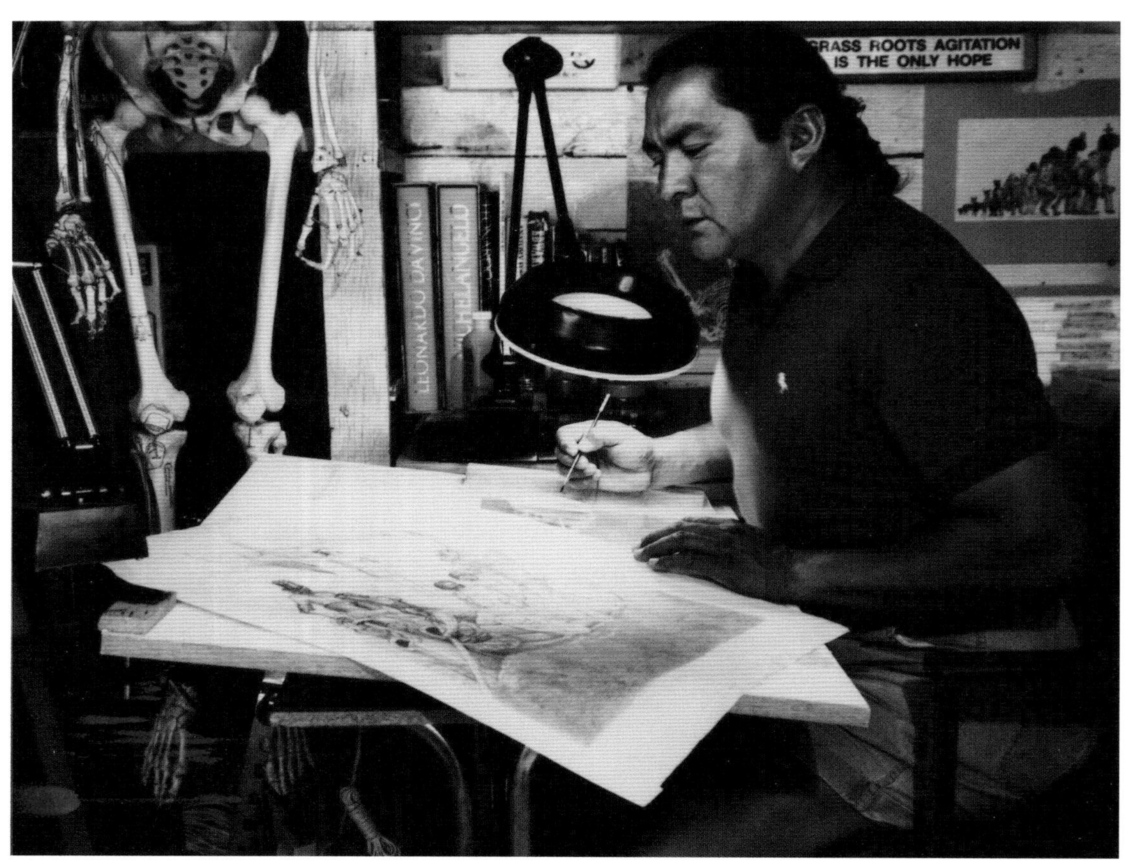

Figure 2. Siegfried Halus, *Floyd Solomon at His Jemez Studio*, 1995.
Gelatin silver print, 7 15⁄16 × 12 5⁄8 in. © Siegfried Halus, courtesy of Maximilian Halus.

INTRODUCTION

400 Years of Remembering and Forgetting

Siegfried Halus

Floyd Raymond Solomon, also known as Tsi-Yuutsi, of Laguna and Zuni origin, was born on April 24, 1952, the son of Calvin and Juanita ("Birdie") Solomon. He grew up on Laguna Pueblo with three brothers and eight sisters, and all were reared with the powerful matriarchal influence of their mother. Floyd's grandfather James Solomon was governor of Laguna when the Laguna Constitution was amended in 1958. It should be noted that this was unusual, as James Solomon was full-blooded Zuni. This meant the family had a heightened involvement in the social and political life of Laguna as well as filial ties to the Zuni Pueblo. In this fertile environment, Floyd and two of his sisters became artists dedicated to Native expressions. Verna Solomon has taught at the Institute of American Indian Arts (IAIA) and is known for contemporary masks and pottery; Sue Dailey is a master of traditional sash weaving. Floyd was their younger brother, and Sue and Verna encouraged him to advance himself artistically.

I met Floyd at the IAIA in Santa Fe, where he enrolled in two of my photography classes from 1990 to 1993. Floyd expressed a genuine and authentic quality that had a seductive impact on all who met him, leaving them with a desire to become friends and colleagues. From the beginning he impressed me as a highly principled individual who was truly motivated and deeply committed to becoming an artist. I was touched by his openness and willingness to engage students and faculty with endless probing questions. I photographed him over a twenty-year period, documenting him with his family and students and occasionally under impromptu circumstances. Floyd was always willing to collaborate photographically, and I was delighted by his ability to generate highly differentiated representations of himself, adapting to unusual environments and introspective moments. His physical appearance was robust, and he was always impeccably dressed: blue jeans, creased in the front, with a pressed shirt and jacket. He had thick black hair, bound in a traditional Pueblo knot that was pulled back tightly, accentuating his broad facial features. When viewed from profile, his demeanor was stoic, presenting a commanding air of authority.

Floyd navigated easily between Pueblo and non-Pueblo worlds, and he had a gift for welcoming everyone he met. Any sense of awkwardness or hesitation would disappear once you gave in to his ribald humor. He could be mischievous and appear vulnerable at the same time, and his mischievousness knew no bounds. Once while visiting a friend at Acoma Pueblo, Floyd encountered a group of German tourists who had just arrived. He followed them on their tour. One of them asked, "What are those freestanding structures on the edge of the mesa?" and Floyd's reply was immediate: "They are meditation booths used by all who live here!" He was convinced that the tourists went back to Germany with the news that Acoma Indians undoubtedly have a highly evolved spiritual life because they have constructed dedicated chambers for meditation. Not for a moment did the tourists suspect their true purpose as outhouses.

A vibrant way of life existed in the Solomon household, encompassing traditional aspects and elements of a non-Native world. During Floyd's childhood his father was often away working for the railroad, and during these absences Floyd's mother, Juanita, would call upon him to carry out many of his father's responsibilities. These increased duties and Juanita's expectations for all her children to pursue higher education and participate in tribal functions set the stage for Floyd's growing interests in Laguna's essential heritage. Floyd would often comment on his childhood at Laguna, including episodes that spoke volumes about tourists who visited the pueblo and how they reacted to contemporary Native life. Floyd witnessed instances in which popular misconceptions were played out and thoughtless stereotyping was expressed. These pointed to a darker sense of how such attitudes came to be: they were linked to a distorted history that failed to recount the cruelty and injustice of those who wished to undo and destroy the cultural and religious integrity of his ancestors.

It is generally acknowledged that personal memories reside in each of us.

They are part of our worldly reality, unlike historic events, which are mostly recorded in books, archives, and countless other temporal forms. Sometimes we are compelled to reexamine historic material, especially during times when cultural forces or moral accountability demand it. On certain occasions new evidence is brought to light, often through individual discoveries, provoking reactions that can alter our perception of history. Floyd Solomon faced just such a dilemma when it became clear to him that the Spanish conquistadors and their missionaries had authored much of what we know about Pueblo history. Numerous documents exist that indicate that Spanish scribes documented Pueblo encounters and armed conflicts objectively. However, often omitted are the accounts of punishing actions against the very foundation of religious life and traditions. Indeed, the Spanish went to great lengths to destroy the Pueblos' language, ceremonies, dancing traditions, and even the heart of their religious practice, the Kiva—building churches on these same sites (which they assumed would lead to conversion to and acceptance of Catholicism). They were pitiless and unyielding in their desire to convert Natives to their one true faith, exploiting this mandate to justify their rapacious hunger for utter domination. Floyd realized that conquered people rarely have a voice in how their history is presented.

When Floyd compared tribal accounts from the rich oral reservoir and recollections of stories told when he was a boy to that of the official history of the dominant culture, he uncovered many contradictions. Ultimate clashes with Spanish and American historical accounts led him to a crossroads. He knew that preceding tribal generations must have come to similar conclusions about the shameful effects of repressed or forgotten facts, but he found that no collective testament had survived.

He was convinced of the need to create artworks to convey essential truths depicting untold suffering and resentment. Floyd could never feel pride in a history laced with negative cultural innuendos and the abdication of Pueblo sovereignty. The message to Native youth and to non-Indians would be this: the cultural amnesia he witnessed on all sides was a heavy price to pay for this disconnection.

This dramatic impact on Floyd would resurface as commentary in his future work. Thus, Floyd determined to bring these submerged narratives forward so that they could become part of the Pueblo tribal legacy. He wanted to create a testament of regained authority for Laguna, in part to enliven the imaginations of Laguna youth drifting from their cultural heart and religious beliefs. His need to correct distortions and biased historical accounts became his raison d'être.

Floyd's path led him beyond his Pueblo community. He served a tour of duty in the US Navy during the Vietnam War, where he grew through his perceptions of other peoples whose way of life was also threatened by dominating forces and imminent change. Floyd's worldview was impacted by his military experience. His identity as a Native American with traditional beliefs and Pueblo upbringing began to fray as he confronted the regimen of US military culture. From the period of enlistment onward he came under extraordinary pressures to fit in. The world he knew at Laguna was clearly his anchor, but while onboard a US Navy vessel in the midst of war he was awash in a world he had not encountered before. As he arrived in different ports he witnessed how some cultures flourished, but he also saw how other traditional cultures and their ways of life were being changed or destroyed. The importance of maintaining his traditions and values became imperative. Upon his return to New Mexico, these memories stirred him to act more decisively. While he enrolled at the University of New Mexico to pursue an accounting degree, the desire to speak truth to Pueblo history persisted. Floyd could no longer ignore his all-consuming ambition to become an artist, so he ultimately abandoned his career in finance. Floyd desperately wanted to be an agent of change, and he made it his mission to reengage Pueblo youth in the authentic ways and values of his people. He wanted to negate apathy and substance abuse, counterbalance the ubiquitous external seductions from non-Indian realms, and inspire the young to embody Pueblo culture and history.

Floyd was becoming increasingly politicized. He found the results of his own research exasperating and surreal: repeated broken promises, exploitation of Pueblo lands, reassignment of Native children to government schools, and the humiliating punishment and physical harm inflicted upon those who spoke their traditional languages—and of course so much more. He took action to denounce the five-hundredth-year celebration of Christopher Columbus by creating a series of posters and silk-screened T-shirts announcing that the First People and their culture had a definitive history that preceded the European invasion. He felt strongly that Native Americans should not participate in honoring Columbus, whose barbaric treatment of Indians was well-known.

Traditional Native cultures have always endured these assaults. In the 1992 exhibition catalog for *The Submuloc Show* ("Columbus" spelled backward), author Lucy R. Lippard vigorously asserts in her commentary about Christopher Columbus that "in spite of knowing for centuries about his horrific policies and immeasurable cruelty, we still honor him." She further writes,

> How come it's taken us so long to turn on Columbus? For years we have raised statues, praised in history books, taught our children to celebrate Columbus Day . . . and all along the Hitlerian facts were known, but not made known: Hatuey burning at the stake, saying that if heaven was where Spaniards went, he would prefer hell. The hands and noses cut off, the gold and blood and forests, the seeds of slavery. The graciously donated blankets infected with smallpox. The treaties/trickeries. And all along, radicals, progressives, liberals, democrats, educators, writers, artists—most of us never took it into our already heavy white-guilt packs. Indigenous genocide is mentioned but never internalized. How many contemporary artists have concerned themselves with the historic theft of lives, land, and culture? Like the atomic bomb, it has been too terrible to picture. Time to change that. For the Post-Columbian World, we need a picture cure. A new history with images that go in through the eyes on a direct line into the heart, which is where resistance begins.

Floyd felt the need to set things right, to create honest and open discourse that would allow his people to face their past and redirect their attention to the voices of the elders. The action of creating artistic work to awaken and shift consciousness was solidly in Floyd's sights.

Inspired by the powerful connection to his family, Floyd began to draw and paint what was most meaningful to him. Drawings and paintings of his mother adorned in traditional dress captured loving portrayals of her that simultaneously illustrated the power of matriarchy. Many family members became his subjects; Floyd found succor in and was driven by his personal experience of Pueblo life. Exploring issues of Native identity fed his budding interest in accurately rendering intimate aspects of Laguna social and traditional life. His earliest drawings attest to the struggle he confronted as he worked to develop his skills as a draughtsman. His determination to master anatomy, perspective, line, tone, drawing, and composition filled his sketchbooks. Untutored and laboring on his own, Floyd made progress by referencing historical images, especially nineteenth- and early twentieth-century photographs depicting life at Laguna. One in particular appealed to him.

It portrayed Laguna women selling traditional pottery to tourists at the Laguna railroad station. Rather than working from the natural environment, he chose to draw from photographs like this that allowed him to scrutinize and render the two-dimensional relationships required in drawing. Bolstered with newfound confidence, and aware that he was finally seeing results and receiving praise and encouragement, he ultimately undertook the narrative depictions of historical injustices to Pueblo people.

Yet he remained unsettled. He often spoke of a crisis among fellow Native artists who no longer felt sustained by traditional Native art-making methods. Floyd revealed that he felt conflicted when trying to execute these narratives within a traditional approach. On one hand, he understood how vital the traditional crafts and stylistic applications were and their importance in preserving cultural meaning and practices, but he also felt driven to create a visual language whose vocabulary could successfully address a broader audience.

Floyd Solomon set himself a task of exploring traditional art-making of Pueblo and non-Pueblo artists—their use of symbolism and stylistic techniques, how they organized the picture plane, and their methods of rendering and production. He persisted in making contact with other Native students and faculty to share his thoughts about a growing number of Native artists who were engaged in a major shift that contested traditional definitions of Native Art. The IAIA seemed at the center of this accelerated rush to explore and experiment within a modernist context. Floyd's favorite expression describing this period was "The New Paradigm." Questioning whether traditional stylistic approaches, which were so dominant in Pueblo art, were too reductive, formulaic, or rigid, he was determined in his search to find sources that offered solutions that went beyond the iconography of his Native tradition. He expressed a desire to consider the possibility of creating an amalgam or fusion of numerous methods. Could his ideas be convincingly communicated to a disparate audience?

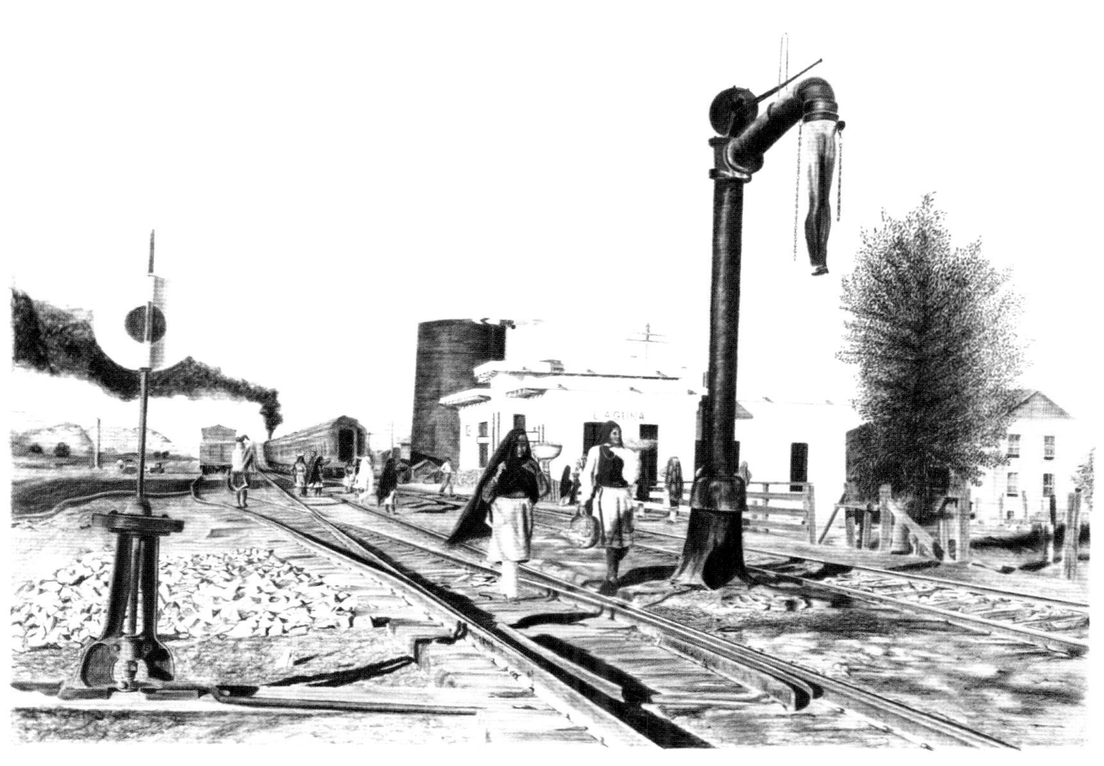

Figure 3. Floyd Solomon, *Laguna Industry*, 1900, 1985. Charcoal on paper, 22 1/2 × 30 in. IAIA Museum of Contemporary Native Arts, Santa Fe, NM, L-42.

Floyd's quest and his continual navigation among different cultural artifacts and stylistic solutions finally freed him to create a remarkable artistic bridge that encompassed Pueblo and non-Pueblo solutions. While examining drawings, prints, and paintings by Rembrandt, Kollwitz, Picasso, and Goya for their consummate drawing skills and gestural clarity, he saw how these works revealed and exposed the cruelty inflicted upon hapless victims—how Europeans had also suffered devastation and suppression. Their works made absolute sense to him. They presented a humane model with expressive techniques that demonstrated sympathetic support for suffering, which he could adapt to express his painful stories. The artists he studied were profoundly committed to producing works with a call to action. Their mission was to name the perpetrators of these hideous crimes in order to expose and create imagery that would blaze into the memory of the people. Floyd consciously constructed a proto-Native and European approach in hopes of insuring that both Indians and non-Indians would receive his message.

Obsessively interested in setting things right, Floyd often said that he would never forgive himself if he did not dedicate his life to revealing what was unsung or forgotten about the Spanish conquest and its impact on his people. He endeavored to accurately portray these stories in an accessible visual system. Dedicating years to formulating and executing these narratives, Floyd envisioned an extensive suite of etchings titled *Crucifixion of a Culture*. He wanted these etchings to become part of the Pueblo cultural stream, having currency and acceptance as important tribal history, a pictorial record born out of Pueblo oral tradition and extensive personal research. For this work he intentionally chose a small 5 × 7 in. format as it demanded closer inspection and established greater viewing intimacy.

He was convinced that his dual role of artist and advocate was necessary in order to stand against deceptive histories. Floyd assigned himself the role of chronicler in order to create documents that would both inform and inspire across generations. In particular, Floyd's passion was directed at Pueblo youth and countering the powerful influences swaying them from their own distinct heritage. He knew they needed to hear, see, and embrace the truth of their history from an Indigenous perspective.

During a careful examination of Floyd's extant etchings, I became aware of a growing sadness in me that extended beyond the time spent viewing his work. It was as if I heard the lamentations of those who suffered so long ago: here at last they were being heard and honored in spite of discarded truth. I realized that these etchings needed to be seen in a broader public arena, and that they would enhance our understanding of how the eras of oppression impacted the Pueblo people. Floyd felt that, historically, fear of repercussions led to what he termed "a behaviorally conditioned response of silence." He said, "The silence is evident not only in Pueblo communities, which often don't talk about the horrors of the past, but also in western depictions of Southwestern history."

Floyd Solomon sought to define his goals as a Pueblo artist by confronting and challenging the anguished legacy of humiliation and cultural destruction. These painful and unresolved resentments have festered for centuries as an open wound that still needs healing. His mission was to communicate honestly with all who encountered his work, be they Native, Hispanic, Anglo, or Asian. The issues raised in Floyd's etchings provoke profound questions and awaken in the viewer the chilling denial of historic complicity that, to the present day, still haunts the American conscience.

In spite of often being unable to secure a consistent source of income, either from sales of his artwork or from commissions, Floyd never lost faith. Financial difficulties forced him to take a hiatus from his project from time to time, and there were personal challenges as well. He had an abiding love for his two children. He was deeply committed to reaching out to them and conflicted by a lack of access to them. This torment often resulted in periods of sadness that affected his emotional and creative life. He began to accept time-consuming jobs that paid little and would siphon off the remaining intervals that he could to devote to *Crucifixion of a Culture*. In these complicated times Floyd sought comfort and solace in traditional Pueblo life, participating in ceremonial dances as he had in the past, seeking advice from elders, and receiving further instruction in the Kiva.

Floyd Solomon's untimely death on November 23, 2008, brought an end to a very promising career and a truly courageous project. He had planned to generate forty-five copperplate etchings depicting distinct episodes in the Spanish and American eras of suppression. In the end, he completed sixteen.

Siegfried Halus
Santa Fe, New Mexico, 2017

CHAPTER 1

The Spanish and the Pueblos

The narrative that Floyd Solomon provided in *Crucifixion of a Culture* draws on both the stories he heard growing up and scholarly accounts. While there are, of course, differing viewpoints, much of the negative history of encounters between Spanish and Native people is clear from the detailed descriptions of actions left by the Spanish themselves. Adamant record keepers, the Spanish who came in more than 130 waves of exploration to the Southeast, Southwest, California, and South America from 1492 to 1598 (Flint 2008, 206) encountered many people and had monumental effects.[1] In the Southwest, Vázquez de Coronado and subsequently Don Juan de Oñate made the most often recounted historical entrees with the greatest impact, ultimately leading to the Pueblo Revolt of 1680; there were, however, many other exploratory ventures. While Coronado was in northern Mexico and the Southwest between 1539 and 1542 and Oñate did not arrive in present-day New Mexico and western Arizona until 1598, the two expeditions were closely connected. Actions taken by Coronado and subsequent Spanish forces, civil authorities, and missionaries in the region, including those of Oñate, led to the growing resistance that resulted in rebellions.[2] Despite Spanish royal

1. Richard Flint has been of immense assistance to me. When he learned about this project, he volunteered to read the brief chapter on the initial Spanish and Pueblo encounters and offered important corrections and suggestions. Richard and Shirley Flint also knew Floyd Solomon and are thus familiar with his goals and the series of images he made that comprise *Crucifixion of a Culture.*

2. Publications concerning the arrival of the Spanish in the Southwest and their encounters with Native people are legion.

proclamations about humane treatment of Indigenous people from as early as the first few years of the sixteenth century, such edicts were regularly ignored.

Recognizing the conduct and impact of the Spanish in the Southwest does not, of course, lead to an overall condemnation of Hispanic culture in the region. Many Spanish settlers intermarried with Pueblos, for example, and others argued for clemency in the face of harsh punishment of Natives. But given the specificity of Spanish accounts, grasping some of the actions that spurred the Pueblo people to revolt is not difficult.

The Spanish faced major difficulties in their attempts to communicate with Pueblo people. Although various leaders came to the region with interpreters, most were ineffectual given the vast diversity of language groups among the Pueblos. With at least five major linguistic divisions and further subgroupings beyond that, expecting the newly encountered people to understand what these strange invaders were saying was almost impossible. Even Franciscan friars made no attempts to learn Native languages. Sign language helped to some extent, but the diversity of Pueblo languages worked to the disadvantage of the Spanish and the benefit of the Pueblos. Pueblo people had a wide understanding of languages among themselves as well as among the Apache and Diné (Wilcox 2009, 103) and could communicate without the Spanish understanding what information was being exchanged. This aspect of Pueblo strategy worked in their favor as they planned various actions against the Spanish, all intended to allow the Pueblo people to retain their cultural identity, practices, and homes.

It is vital to acknowledge that Pueblo people, and other Native people as well, took important steps to ensure their cultural survival. The Spanish, while offering detailed descriptions of clothing and villages, for example, did not initially provide records of masked dances (Flint 2008, 180), and later Pueblo

---

While pueblo author Joe Sando wrote of the Pueblo Revolt that its "story is one familiar to all Americans" (1998, 3), I have not found this to be true. That said, this chapter in no way aspires to either present a comprehensive view of information provided elsewhere nor to offer new examinations of the era of the sixteenth and seventeenth centuries in Tierra Nueva. It is intended, quite simply, to provide some background for those readers unfamiliar with the essential history of this period and a foundation for the images that Floyd Solomon created, which are the central focus of this study.

people kept their dances away from prying eyes. Pueblos sustained many of their important cultural and religious activities in the midst of Spanish colonial efforts to destroy them. In many other ways Pueblos maintained their identity, even abandoning villages to avoid additional contact with the Spanish and their Mexican Native allies. As Wilcox (2009) and others convincingly argue, these "abandonments" were not solely the drastic result of disease but were, instead, consciously taken as part of a continuing strategy. While at times Pueblos faced marauding Apache and Diné people, at other times in their attempts to avoid destruction by the Spanish these various people became allies (Carter 2009, 138–208). These alliances were pivotal throughout the late sixteenth and seventeenth centuries.

The pueblos did not, of course, contain the great wealth that false reports had suggested. The Spanish kept looking, however. What they did not know was the location of some minerals that were of essential importance to the Pueblo people but not to the Spanish. The location of turquoise, for example, was apparently kept secret as it is not mentioned in the documents from Coronado's expedition. This, as well as no early records of masked dances even though the Spanish were well aware of kivas or ritual spaces, underscores some of the careful ways in which the Pueblo people protected both their ritual observances and such valuables as turquoise from the Spanish. As much as possible it seems that initially the Pueblo people avoided the Spanish by leaving their villages when they knew the outsiders were approaching.

Most of the men who arrived with Coronado or Oñate or other expeditionary leaders were not wealthy but hoped to gain from a practice of taxation—the encomienda system—that would allow them to levy tariffs on the Native people they controlled. However, perhaps two thousand of Coronado's force were actually Native allies from what is now Mexico (Flint 2009, 73). The Mexican Native would have been accompanied by slaves and women as was custom (Flint 2017). These were extremely capable warriors for whom battle with other Native people brought value and reward beyond a purely monetary one, as their stature and position could increase with successes in war against worthy adversaries, and prisoners might be taken.

The Spanish also brought horses and large dogs, and later sheep, goats, cattle, and, of course, guns, none of which the Pueblo people had. Although the

Spanish had these advantages, their guns and crossbows were initially unable to ward off Pueblo people during battle. The bows and arrows of the Pueblos, and in some locations the strategic use of stones, were far more effective (Flint 2008, 84). Pueblo people did, however, use some weapons and armor that had been captured in various battles.

On July 7, 1540, the Spanish expeditionary forces, under Coronado's command, arrived at the Zuni village of Hawikku, one of the famed cities of Cibola. Zuni or Shiʾwana, located between present-day Albuquerque, New Mexico, and the Hopi mesas in Arizona, may have been the inspiration for Fray Marcos de Niza's earlier 1538–1539 extravagantly inflated accounts of the wealth to be found in the area.

Even though Coronado initially led more than 2,800 soldiers and Native warriors, slaves, and women, he had come north to Zuni with a much smaller force. The people of Zuni refused to let them enter their village. A battle ensued, and the Spanish and their allies captured the pueblo. Smaller parties explored beyond Zuni, reaching the Hopi mesas to the west and Acoma to the east. The Spanish and their allies visited Acoma as well as Hopi. Continuing their exploration, they reached Tiguex, a large pueblo in the region of present-day Albuquerque, and the Spanish also explored other pueblos including Pecos.

Spanish forces were unprepared for the winter of 1540–1541, an extremely harsh one. They traded for supplies and blankets or simply took them. By this stage there were various accusations of mistreatment of the Pueblos, including the rape of women, while other men were held captive and sometimes tortured in an attempt to induce them to reveal the location of gold. These incidents and others led to increased resentment. The Tiguex War of 1540–1541 resulted. Sieges of about twelve Tiwa villages occurred. While losses were significant on both sides, at least fifty Tiwa men were burned at the stake for idolatry. Despite the war, Coronado continued to send men to explore other pueblos including those of Zia and Jemez.

Franciscan friars stayed in the region in hopes of converting the Pueblo people, but Coronado ultimately returned to Mexico in 1542. Following the establishment of additional laws in Spain pertaining to the treatment of Native people, an investigation of Coronado's actions against Pueblos occurred between 1544 and 1546 that resulted in allegations that, among other things, Coronado had ordered his men to set dogs on people, had excessively executed Pueblos without cause, and had ultimately failed to settle Tierra Nueva. Although the allegations were not proven, witnesses did not deny them, though they could not agree upon whose orders actions were taken (Flint 2002; Flint 2008, 166–67).

While other explorers followed and harsh treatment of Native people continued, it was not until the late 1580s that any substantial additional Spanish movement began. In some cases, they encountered abandoned villages where memories of Coronado's previous attacks were strong. The Spanish needed provisions and took both food and clothing as well as pottery that they found.

Battles continued in parts of Nuevo Mexico as winter weather encroached and the Spanish found themselves once again ill-equipped. Denied entrance to Pecos Pueblo in December of 1590, the Spanish battled the Pueblo people, defeated them, and remained among the Pueblos for several months. The leader of this expedition, Castaño de Sosa, had not obtained permission from the viceroy in Mexico for his journey and was subsequently arrested, tried, and convicted. In order to circumvent this type of illegal exploration and others that followed shortly thereafter, the viceroy gave Juan de Oñate the exclusive right to settle New Mexico.

Leaving Mexico in January 1598, Oñate and nearly six hundred setters in addition to Native allies came north. A small delegation accompanied Oñate to Santo Domingo (Kewa) Pueblo, where he took two men as interpreters. He called a council with the seven nearby pueblos and, through the interpreters, asked the representatives to pledge allegiance to Spain, clearly assuming the Pueblo people understood what they were pledging. Oñate's entrance into the region also resulted in the establishment of permanent missions.

Oñate moved north from Santo Domingo and, as winter approached again, he both traded and took food from the Pueblos he encountered, leaving those communities low on food for themselves. As was the case from the beginning of Spanish presence in the Southwest, the taxation of the people in the form of large quantities of corn as well as other food and blankets left the Pueblo people without sufficient supplies. The region was at the end of a severe drought (Carter 2009, 145). That reality notwithstanding, if Pueblos could not supply the large amount of corn required of them, the Spanish system of *repatimiento* (servitude) resulted until the required encomienda tribute could be supplied.

The people of Acoma, atop their 365-foot mesa, had had enough, and they plotted to kill Oñate. But Oñate sensed a trap and was able to leave with his men. Before he left, however, he had sent word for his nephew, Juan de Zaldiar, to join him, and, after learning that his nephew had been killed at Acoma along with several others, the Spanish under Oñate's orders attacked and captured the pueblo. Many people were burned alive in the kivas and in their homes (Hammond and Rey 1953, 2: 614). Captain Luis Gasco de Velasco also reported to the viceroy in Mexico that more than six hundred Acomas had been killed and at least another six hundred taken as prisoners (Hammond and Rey 1953, 2: 615). Despite pleas for clemency from various colonists, captives were tried at Santo Domingo, and Oñate ordered that twenty-four men over a period of twenty-five years would have one of their feet amputated; they were sentenced to twenty years of servitude. Younger men between twelve and twenty-five years of age were also sentenced to twenty years as slaves, as were women over twelve. Two Hopi men who had been at Acoma and had joined in the battle had one of their hands cut off; they were sent home to their pueblo as a warning to the Hopi people. If their parents had taken part in the uprising, girls under the age of twelve were placed under the guidance of Fray Alonso Martinez, and boys of the same age were under the military supervision of Vincente de Zaldivar (Hammond and Rey 1953, 1: 477–78). While Spanish settlements increased widely during Oñate's tenure, he ultimately resigned as governor in 1609 and was exiled for his harsh treatment of Native people.

The era following Oñate's was one in which church and civil authorities disagreed in various ways. Franciscan friars wanted their missions to be exempt from taxes, for example, while the civil government felt the encomienda tribute was rightly theirs for providing protection to the missions. The Pueblos were well aware of these conflicts. Even though various Pueblo people were converted to Catholicism, most retaining their own native religious practices as well, many Pueblos openly rejected the friars and their message. Both missionaries and Spanish civil authorities treated Natives harshly. As a result, armed rebellions occurred throughout the decades following Oñate's departure. One in 1675 at San Juan (Ohkay Owingeh), where three or four Pueblo men were hung, each in his own village (Sando 1998, 11), and some forty others imprisoned, was a key factor in the organization of the much larger, better coordinated, and far more effective revolt five years later. One of the men who had been imprisoned was Popé (Po'pay).

The Pueblo Revolt was the direct result of long-term Pueblo resentment over harsh punishment, widespread mistreatment, excessive taxation, enslavement, and continuing attempts to destroy Pueblo lifeways and beliefs. Even so, not all Pueblo people supported the 1680 revolt, with some giving advance notice to the Spanish of the planned actions; a few of these Pueblo people escaped south with the Spanish at the time of the revolt.

In 1680, however, multiple pueblos united in their bid to force the Spanish from New Mexico. The violence that had resulted from Spanish arrival in the region, which had included severe punishments and even burning Pueblos alive, was intended to serve as a warning in combination with heavy taxation and enslavement but led to a unified movement to force the Spanish from Pueblo land. Popé, the San Juan leader who had taken part in the 1675 revolt and was imprisoned by the Spanish, together with the other remaining captive insurgents, was to be sold into slavery. However, a delegation of Pueblos came to Santa Fe to demand their release. Then-governor Juan Francisco Treviño, perhaps sensing an imminent attack should he refuse, acceded to their request (Kessel 1987, 226–27). Rather than staying at San Juan, Popé went to Taos following his release, and it was from there that the plans for the revolt were finalized. The well-organized, pan-pueblo alliance grew in size and strength through multiple meetings among the leaders of various pueblos including Santo Domingo, Tesuque, Santa Clara, San Ildefonso, Picuris, Taos, and Pecos, among others (Wilcox 2009, 152–53). Recognizing that Spanish supplies would be low in early August, this seemed the perfect time to strike.

Runners between pueblos carried communications about the date for the actual revolt. Each had a knotted rope, and one knot was to be untied each morning until the last was gone; then the rebellion would begin on August 10. Spanish colonists as well as civil and religious authorities were told to leave the villages in advance of the actual attack; some did while others did not. Santa Fe, the colonial capital, was under siege, and the water supply was blocked, thus forcing the Spanish governor and his forces to abandon the city.

Following the revolt, Popé and others encouraged the Pueblos to return to their precolonial lifeways, including using their original names rather than the baptismal ones the Spanish had given them and maintaining their traditional beliefs, ceremonies, and practices. Much as the friars and Spanish soldiers had destroyed Pueblo kivas and ceremonial objects, now Pueblos demolished churches, other mission buildings, and Catholic ritual articles including crosses, images, and rosaries (Hackett 1942, 235, 247–48; Wilcox 2009, 154–58).

Unification of the various pueblos did not continue long after the revolt. Once the oppressors were gone, such a confederation was unnecessary. Each pueblo reestablished its traditional practices without interference from outsiders. While the Spanish made some forays back into the region over the next few years, only beginning in 1692 with forces under Don Diego de Vargas were they able to attempt once again to bring what is now New Mexico under Spanish rule. Multiple additional rebellions, including those of 1694 and 1696, occurred in what was a continual bloody attempt to reestablish control. The Spanish were ultimately allowed to return only after the Pueblos deemed the results of negotiations with them satisfactory.

CHAPTER 2

Modern Native Representations of the Arrival of the Spanish and the Pueblo Revolt

Floyd Solomon's visual record of the arrival and impact of the Spanish in the Pueblo world was his own dynamic personal expression. It was based on stories he had heard as a young boy, supplemented by what he had learned since. While he never purported to represent the views of all Native people or even those of his own specific pueblos, his narrative is a vital one that allowed him to not only know his culture and its history better but to grow in strength as an artist. What is perhaps most surprising is that there are relatively few other works of art by Native artists from the time that Solomon worked—or before or even after—that address the arrival of the Spanish in the Southwest, the history of the encounters that followed, the Pueblo Revolt, and the return of the Spanish.

While most of Solomon's works are not concretely dated, they cover the era from the early 1990s until shortly before his death in 2008. Among the key events that occurred during the early years of his project was the 1992 celebration of the five hundredth anniversary of Christopher Columbus's arrival in Native North America. 1992 was a time when mainstream museums and galleries provided unparalleled opportunities for contemporary Native artists to exhibit their work. Many artists wondered if they would be so popular after that anniversary year ended; in general, the answer to that query is no. Exhibitions from 1992 included at least some works that addressed the arrival of the Spanish, most from regions that had direct contact with conquistadors but others that did not. Rick Rivet (b. 1949), a First Nations artist of Metis descent, painted an extremely powerful large-scale view of a conquistador in armor, wielding a sword, standing in front of a series of white crosses. The ground on which he stands is filled with skulls; the background is blood red. The conquistador's face appearing beneath his helmet is that of a wild boar. Rivet's primary message, about the lack of humanity exhibited by the Spanish soldiers and the results of their entry into the Americas, is clear.

Rivet's work was part of a 1992 exhibition entitled *Indigena, Contemporary Native Perspectives in Canadian Art* organized by the then Canadian Museum of Civilization, now called the Canadian Museum of History, in Hull, Quebec. Curated by Gerald McMaster (Plains Cree) and Lee-Ann Martin (Mohawk), the exhibition brought together the work of sixteen artists "to examine and address such issues as discovery, colonization, cultural critique and tenacity" (McMaster and Martin 1992, 15). Artists created works exploring the residential school system and the continuing effects of colonization, for example. While several others did address the arrival of Columbus and its immediate aftereffects, Rivet's was the most strongly connected to the impact of the Spanish on the Southwest.

Jaune Quick-to-See Smith, an artist of Salish and Kootenai descent, also curated a 1992 exhibition, *The Submuloc Show / Columbus Wohs*. The show, organized by ATLATL, an organization located in Phoenix, Arizona, that promoted Native arts, included work by thirty-three Native artists, including Floyd Solomon; his *Deceptus Magnus* (fig. 18) appeared on the cover of the catalogue and in the exhibition. Some of the works in the show subtly engaged the issues of the quincentennial while others, like Solomon's and Jean LaMarr's (b. 1945, Paiute/Pit River), were more clearly confrontational. LaMarr's installation work *Seven from Hell* includes an etching of seven bust-length figures. The first figure in the print is Columbus, followed by a priest, then a harlot who LaMarr equates to a lost soul. A pimp who represents a businessman is then followed by the murderer, here suggesting Custer. The sixth figure, the thief, is Andrew Jackson, who stole land from the Cherokee, and the seventh figure is the devil, complete with horns (*The Submuloc Show* 1992).

The footwear, in large part, coordinates with the identity of the figures above. The harlot's shoes are clearly the pink high heels while Custer and Jackson both have boots with red pigment to relay their close association with blood and death. Both the priest and the devil are linked through their sandals. A single pair of tan boots, more highly polished than any of the other

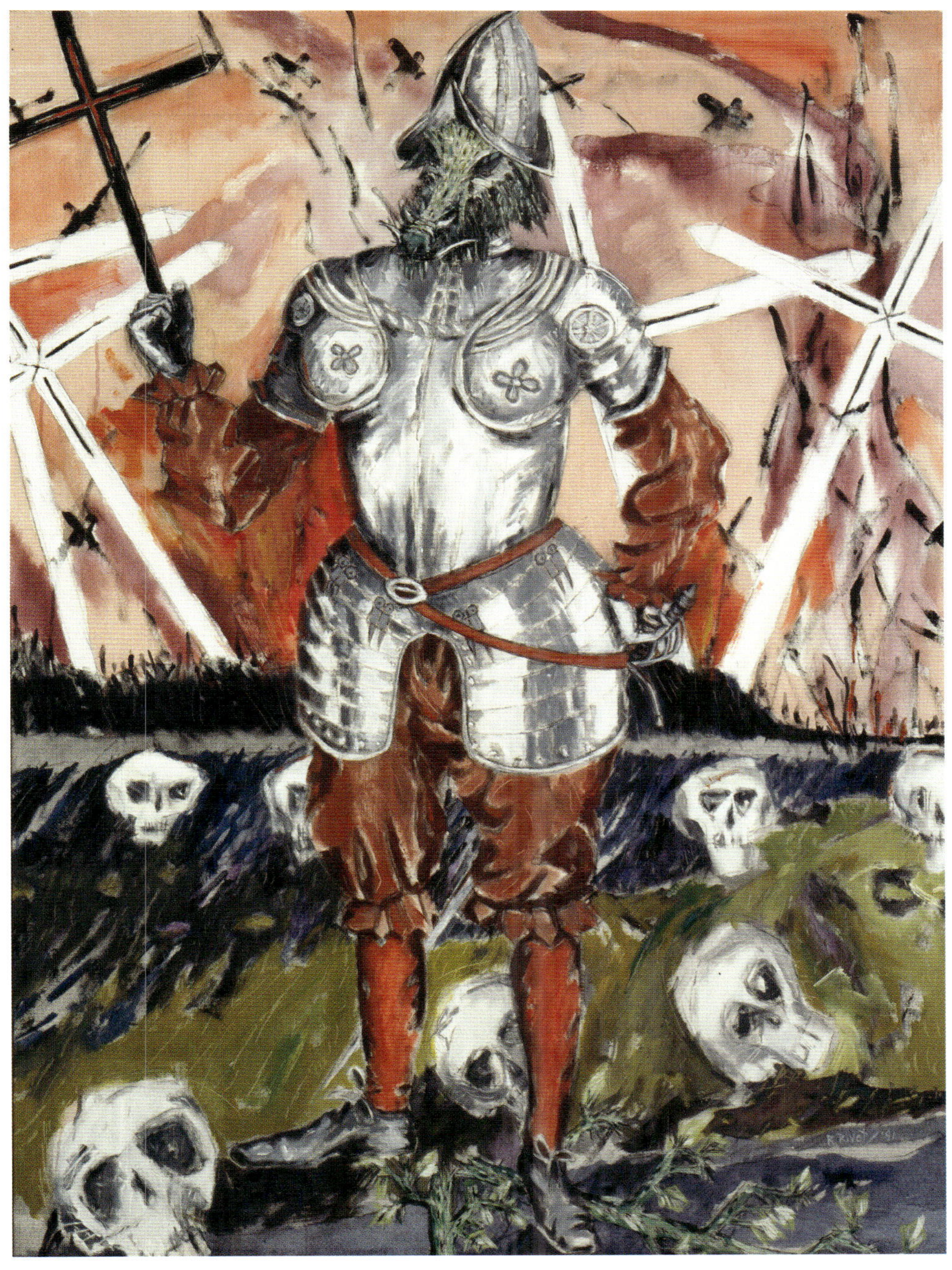

Figure 4. Rick Rivet, Metis, *Legacy*, 1991. Acrylic on canvas, 168 ½ cm × 122 cm. Image courtesy of the Canadian Museum of History, Gatineau, QC.

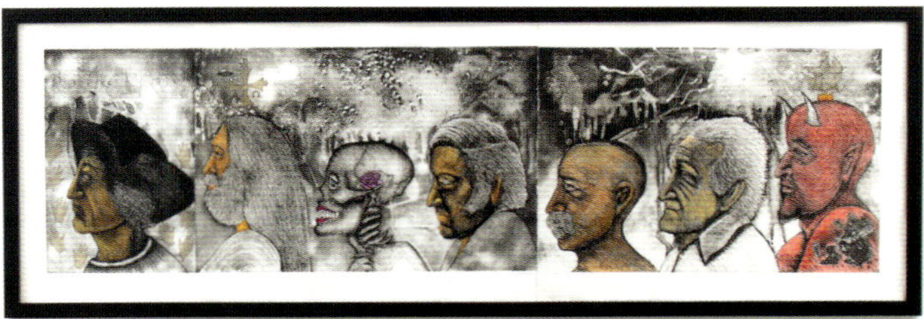

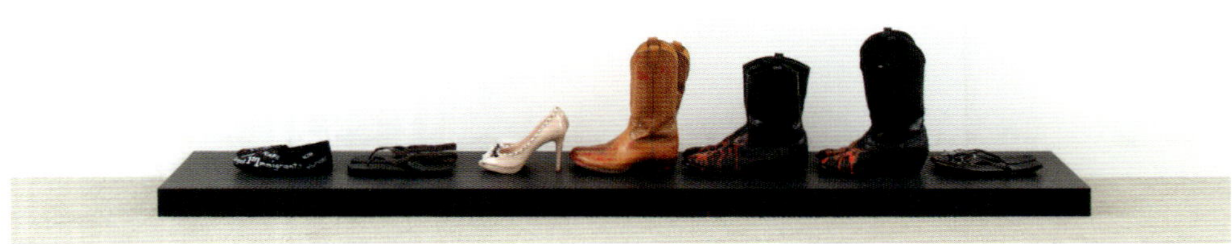

Figure 5. Jean LaMarr, Paiute / Pit River, *Seven from Hell*, undated. Mixed media, 29 ½ × 92 ½ in. Image courtesy of the Crocker Art Museum, Sacramento, CA.

male shoes, represents the smooth businessman that LaMarr associates with a pimp.

Bob Haozous (b. 1943), an artist of Chiricahua and Diné descent, has also created work that references the effects of Spanish arrival in the Southwest. His most powerful is the approximately 17 1/2-foot-tall *Discoverer* from 1991, which elevates a mounted conquistador atop two bases to which are welded cut-out handless bodies and severed hands. The work thus makes specific reference to Don Juan de Oñate's infamous actions concerning Acoma Pueblo where, in the late sixteenth century, he ordered that the people of the pueblo be punished for battling the Spanish. One foot of every Acoma man determined to have been part of that encounter was amputated; some men had hands amputated as well.

That these works came near the 1992 quincentennial is not surprising. Despite their personal reasons for creation, these artists, in part, shared in an important response to that "celebration," a celebration that was not a positive one for Native people. Additional visual artists explored the topic

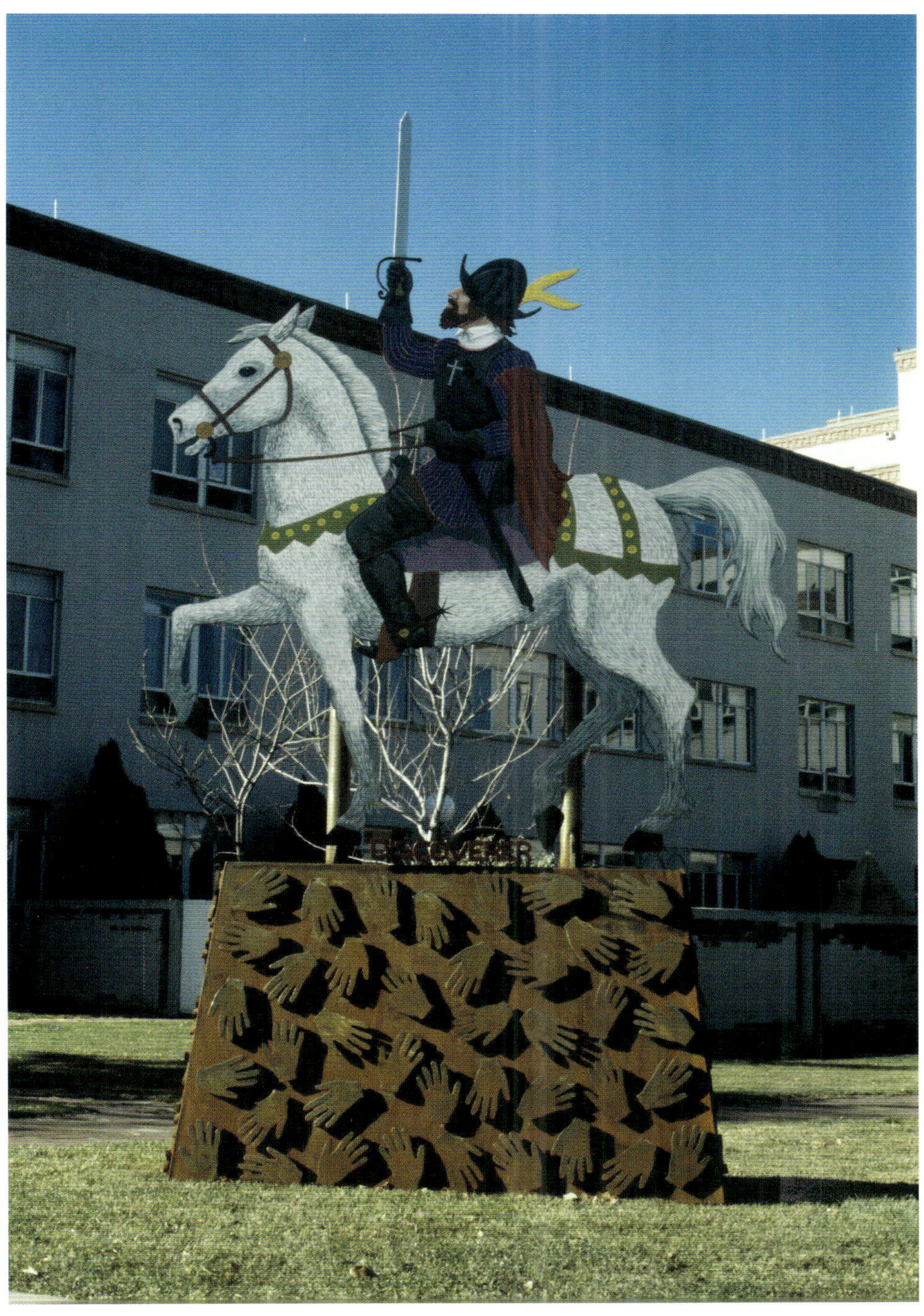

Figure 6. Bob Haozous, *Chiricahua Apache and Diné*, Discoverer, 1991. Welded steel and pigment, 14 ft. 6 in. high. Image courtesy of the artist.

of conflict between Native and Spanish forces in other ways. In both Santa Fe and Albuquerque, New Mexico, alternate views were expressed during celebrations of anniversaries of the founding of New Mexico. In 2005, two artists—one of Hispanic heritage and the other Anglo—were invited to create a collaborative work celebrating the four hundredth anniversary of the "settling" of New Mexico; they subsequently created a work marking Don Juan de Oñate's entrance into the region. Complaints were lodged that there was no Native view of that pivotal event. Nora Naranjo Morse (b. 1953) from Santa Clara Pueblo, a well-known multimedia artist, ultimately created an earthwork *Numbe Whageh* (Our Center Place) that relays the Pueblo connection to the land through raised earth spirals and regional plants that stand in stark contrast to the large-scale bronze figural group representing Oñate, his entourage, and the foreign practices and animals they brought

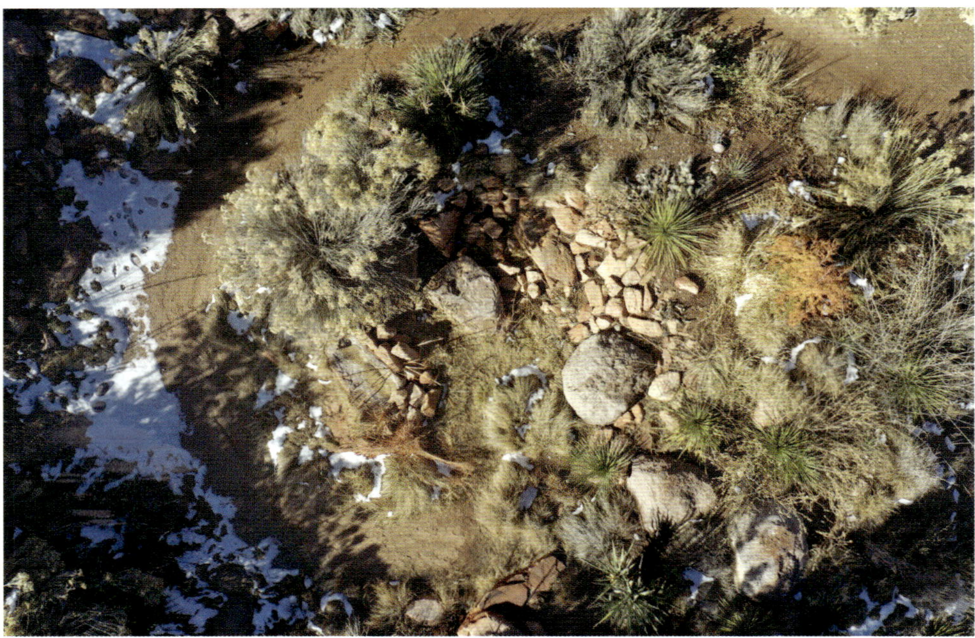

Figure 7. Nora Naranjo Morse, *Santa Clara Pueblo, Numbe Whageh,* 2005. Earthen work. 140 to 157 ft. 1% for the Arts Fund, City of Albuquerque. PAC.058302. Image courtesy of Zakary Naranjo Morse.

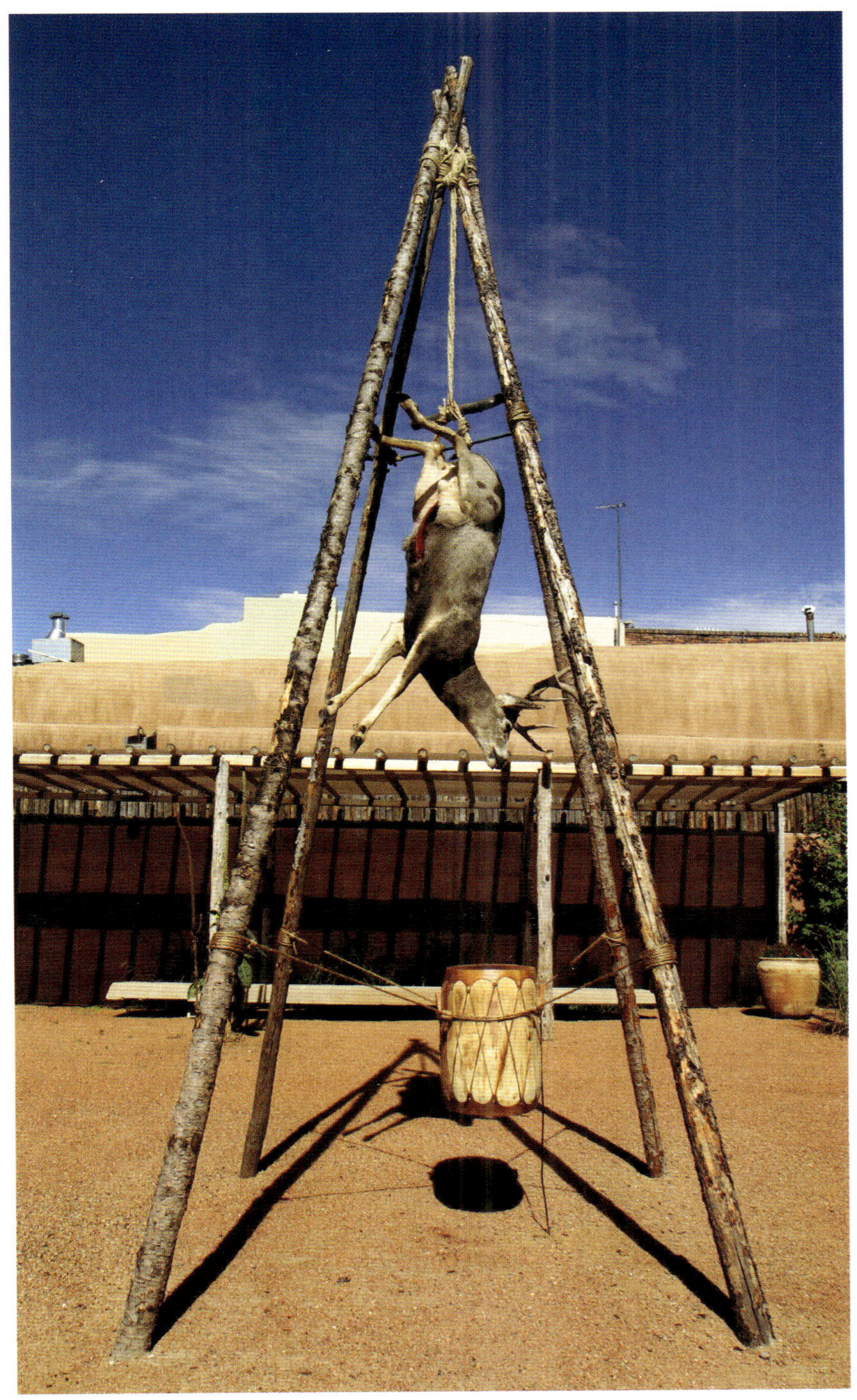

Figure 8. Postcommodity, *My Blood is in the Water,* 2010. Mixed Media, 15 ft. high. Image courtesy of Postcommodity and Bockley Gallery, Minneapolis, MN.

into the Southwest. Naranjo-Morse's work is a peaceful, contemplative suggestion of what life was like prior to the arrival of the Spanish.

In 2010 the artists' collective Postcommodity was commissioned to create a work, *My Blood Is in the Water,* as an Indigenous response to the celebration of the four hundredth anniversary of the founding of Santa Fe. The work included a mule deer's carcass suspended from a wooden tripod over a drum. The red-colored water from the deer struck the drumhead and created not only sound and a rhythm but also a continuous sense of time passing.

The group viewed the work both as a recognition of the way in which Native people traditionally found food as well as a critique of contemporary convenience and processed food. Above all, however, the dripping blood and animal's body underscored the impact of the advent of the Spanish in the area. Both Naranjo-Morse's and Postcommodity's works discussed here, in very different ways, reference the impact of the *entrada.*

Each of the works examined above are powerful single works, not a series like Solomon's. Harry Fonseca (1946–2006), an artist of Maidu heritage, created an abstract but extremely impactful series of images that stands out in this history. Entitled *The Discovery of Gold and Souls in California,* these 160 small, mixed-media paintings combine minerals, including mica, with other materials from the area where gold was discovered in 1848 in Sutter Creek, not far from Maidu territory. The series begins with idyllic landscape images from the area that turn more and more claustrophobic with heavier applications of mica. Red starts to trickle into the landscape, suggesting the blood that was beginning to be shed as prospectors savagely attacked Native people in their way. Several paintings depict crosses with rich blacks and reds often splashed across the paper. One includes a red handprint overlaying the basic cross and black imagery. Despite the lack of human representation, the suggestions are clear. Dated between 1991 and 1992, the works not only fit within the quincentennial year but also temporarily overlap, in part, with some of Solomon's etchings. That Fonseca was from California, where the Spanish mission system had an intense and deadly impact, as did the way in which gold prospectors treated Native people, lends his prints a variant focus but one connected nonetheless to Solomon's.

Floyd Solomon wrote about Fonseca's work for the small catalogue *Floyd Solomon: Earth, Wind, and Fire,* which accompanied an installation at the

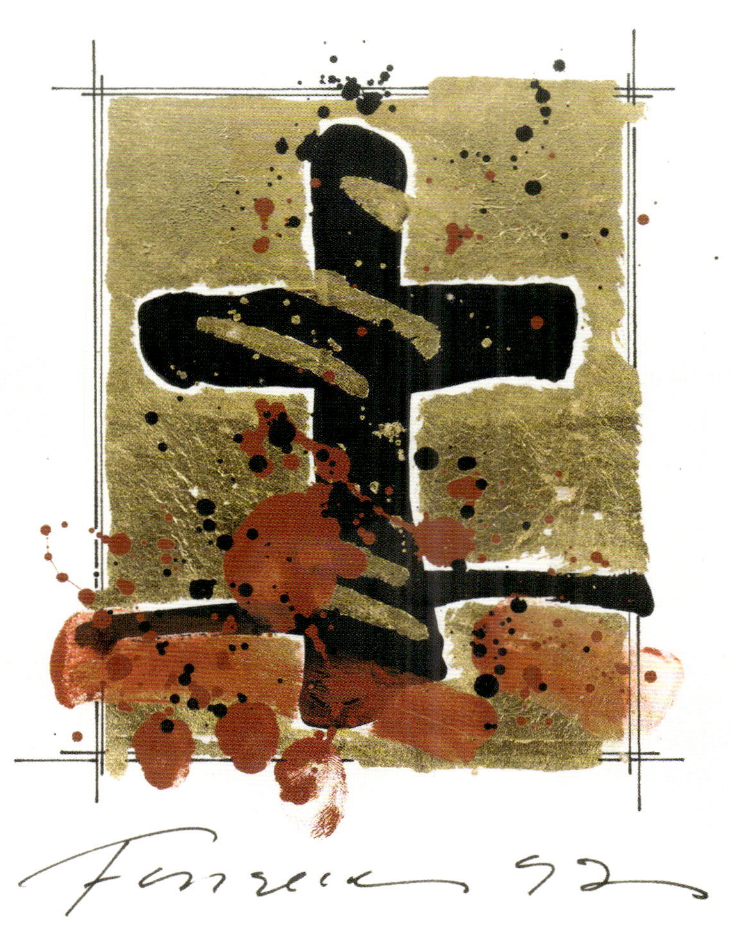

Figure 9. Harry Fonseca, Maidu, *The Discovery of Gold and Souls in California*, 1992. Mixed media painting, 2 ¾ × 15 in. Oakland Museum of California, Oakland, California, 2007.89.11. © Harry Fonseca Collection, Autry Museum of the American West, Los Angeles, CA.

Wheelwright Museum in Santa Fe in 1996: "For Native American communities, the search for the past, through both written and oral history, has led to the discovery of truths, often painful, which influenced their present circumstances. For many individuals, the retracing of cultural history has challenged them to decide whether to turn away from the discovery of truth or proceed to unearth identity" (Solomon 1996, 34).

After discussing the way in which many contemporary Native artists create what the market wants in styles they expect, Solomon noted that Fonseca was an exception: "In his most recent work, he has brought the issue of genocide of indigenous cultures to the fore. . . . He has addressed genocide as a historical event. . . . The array of crosses (symbols of crucifixion) symbolizes the imposition of a foreign belief system in earlier historical times. Do the horizontal extensions of the cross reflect the outstretched arms of a person awaiting salvation, or the empty apparatus of torture awaiting a victim?" (Solomon 1996, 34). Solomon also noted that Fonseca had experience in both the reservation environment and the urban one, much as he did. "He offers an uncommon perspective to Indian communities which serves to inform them of historic events, of which most would have limited knowledge or acceptance. Fonseca has discovered those painful truths . . . and he has communicated them through a visual language which is intelligible to everyone" (Solomon 1996, 35). The author might just as well have been writing about himself as about Fonseca; the aims of the two artists were clearly aligned.

Before the 1990s few contemporary artists appear to have explored subject matter that touched on the negative impact of the Spanish in the Southwest. An intriguing exception to this is found in Hopi artist Fred Kabotie's (1900–1986) untitled 1976 painting, rendered in a manner reminiscent of the 1930s Studio style promoted by Dorothy Dunn at the Santa Fe Indian School. The image depicts a church on Pueblo land being destroyed with a priest suspended over wood about to be ignited by a Pueblo man. Kabotie had a long and distinguished career during which he depicted many genre scenes of Pueblo life, but I know of no other images by him of this type of subject matter. 1976 is also early for such a powerful visual statement against, in this case, Catholicism. That year was, however, the bicentennial year for the United States, and that, like 1992 and its celebrations, probably encouraged Kabotie's selection of subject and graphic presentation.

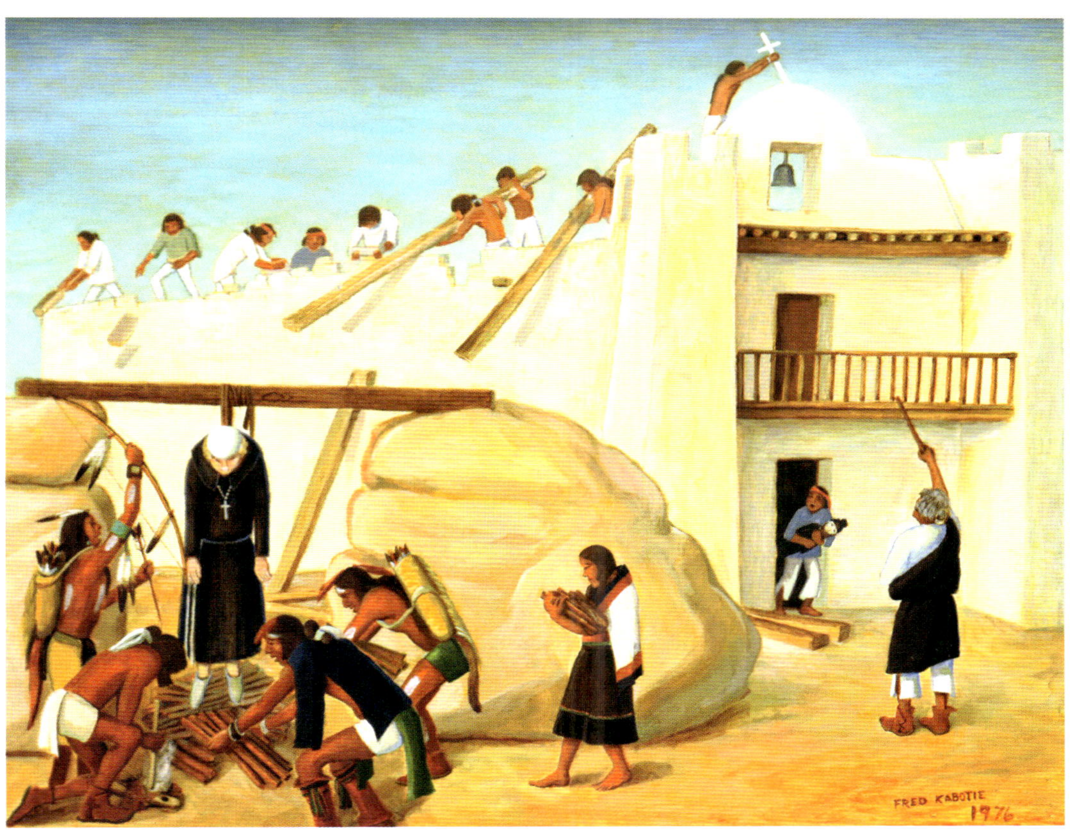

Figure 10. Fred Kabotie, Hopi, *1680 Pueblo Revolt at Hopi*, 1976. Watercolor on illustration board, 16 1/8 × 20 1/16 in. The Museum of Indian Arts and Culture / Laboratory of Anthropology, Santa Fe, NM, 54019/13.

However, there is a priest-killer kachina *tihu* carved by various contemporary Hopi sculptors. The representations of these spirits who live in the San Francisco peaks and bring rain to the Hopi people are given two concrete forms—one as masked dancers when the spirits are in the village and the other as smaller-scale sculpted forms. Originally only made for internal use to allow younger Hopi to begin to recognize the pantheon of spirits, many tihus began to be made for outside sale in the late nineteenth century. The priest killer is said to have appeared shortly after the arrival of the Spanish. The Hopi, adamant in their response to attempts to force them to convert to Catholicism, burned churches and killed priests who would not leave. Tihus vary in specifics, although all contemporary priest-killer representations include a blade carried in one hand and sometimes a head in the other. Thus Kabotie's painting has a firm basis in Hopi culture.

Students at the Institute of American Indian Arts, which literally rose on the grounds of the Santa Fe Indian School in 1962, were, by then, exploring many styles and divergent subjects, having moved strongly away from the Studio style of painting and imagery. But Kabotie was not associated with the IAIA, nor had he been at Dunn's Studio, and he was, by that time, living at Hopi away from the rarified atmosphere of Santa Fe.

Three contemporary Pueblo artists, however, stand out for their repeated exploration of the effects of the Spanish entrada, the 1680 Pueblo Revolt, and the 1692 Spanish return to the region. Two are from Cochiti Pueblo and the third is from Santa Clara.

Jason Garcia (b. 1973), a Tewa ceramic artist, grew up at Santa Clara learning from his parents, who also work with ceramics. His own art, while including ceramic bowls and jars, has focused since 2002 on clay tiles with painted imagery and has recently centered more on printmaking; he completed his MFA in printmaking at the University of Wisconsin–Madison in 2016. Fired clay tiles with abstract designs have a long history in Pueblo ceramics, and Garcia has taken the art form further by using it as a way to recall history and comment on contemporary life. Some of his narrative tiles reference the presence of Po' pay, or Popé, the man from Ohkay Owingeh Pueblo generally credited with organizing the Pueblo Revolt. Other images depict runners carrying or passing a knotted cord to others, the cord used as a time-marking device to let all know when the revolt would begin.

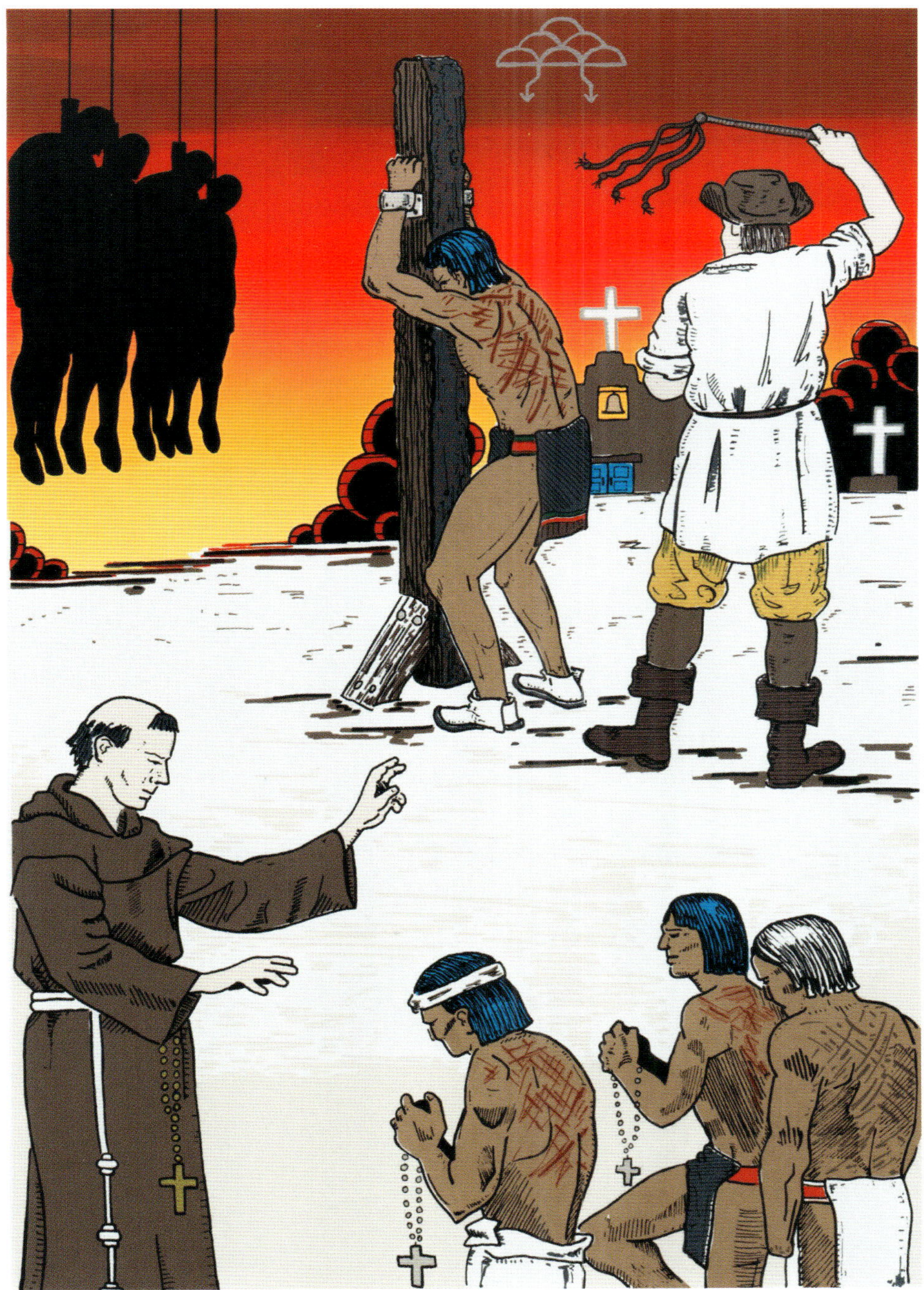

Figure 11. Jason Garcia, Santa Clara Pueblo, *If This Be Doomsday*, from *Tewa Tales Of Suspense!* 2016. Serigraph, ca. 24 × 19 in. University of New Mexico Art Museum, Albuquerque, NM, 2017.1.2. Image courtesy of Geistlight Photography, Albuquerque, NM.

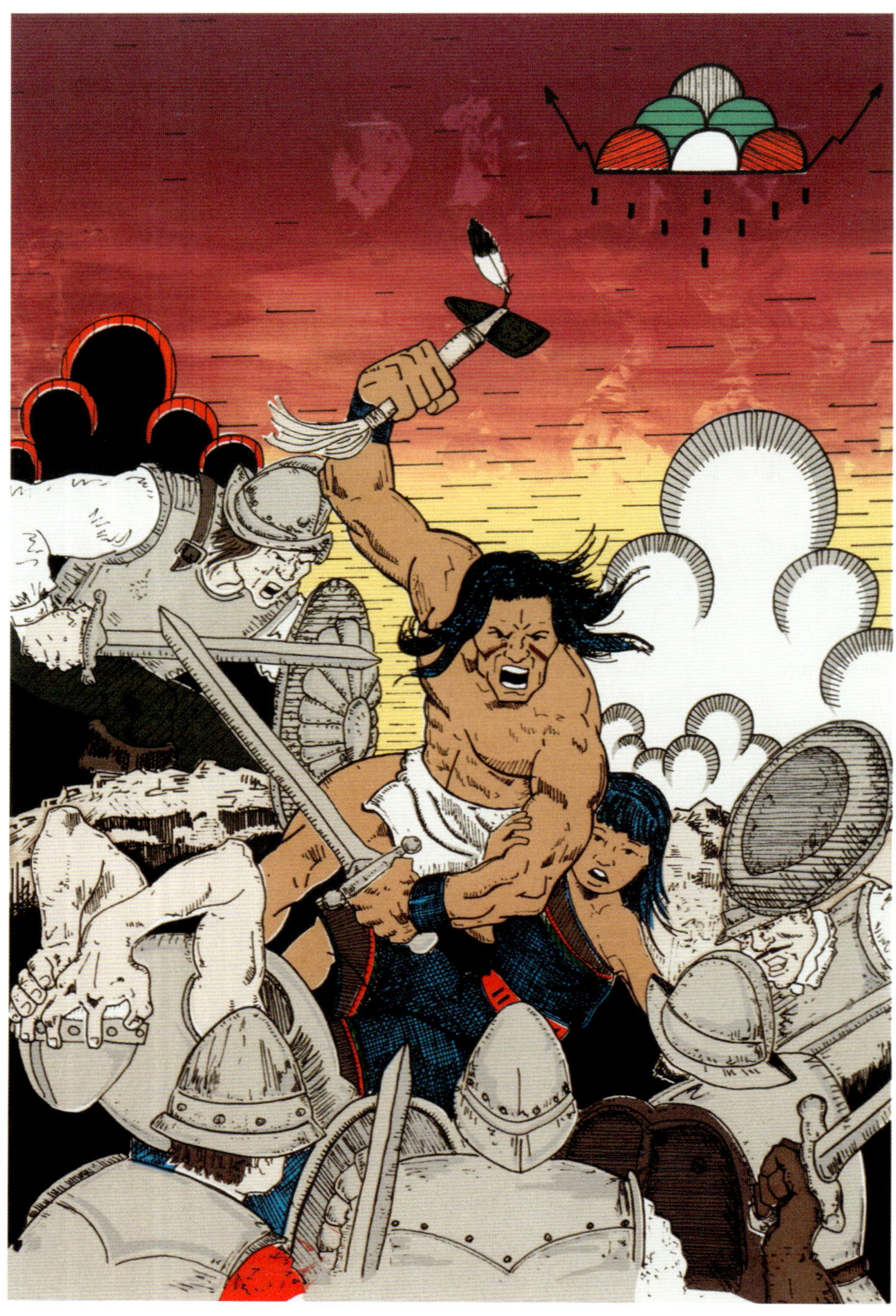

Figure 12. Jason Garcia, Santa Clara Pueblo, *To Conquer a Colossus,* from *Tewa Tales Of Suspense!* 2016. Serigraph, 24 × 19 in. University of New Mexico Art Museum, Albuquerque, NM, 2017.1.5. Image courtesy of Geistlight Photography, Albuquerque, NM.

Garcia began using a painting style on his ceramics years ago that reflects his knowledge of the language of graphic novels or comic-book illustration. While some of his images do suggest humor, these associated with the entrada clearly do not. All are rendered in a boldly outlined style with flat application of natural clay pigment. Some of the images incorporate text balloons and bold titles to further enhance the messages he relays. His print series *Tewa Tales of Suspense* are the most well-known of his entrada-related images. Here he combines Pueblo history with graphic-novel superheroes, bringing cultural heroes from the past into the present. His are readily accessible narratives that speak to young people as well as older ones. A seven-print series from *Tewa Tales,* his final MFA project, illustrates several episodes of Spanish encounters with Pueblo people. Here there are no additional text balloons; the prints and their titles effectively relay the story. *If This Be Doomsday!* presents a friar with three Pueblo men, each showing signs of torture with scars on their bodies. Two kneel and hold rosaries while the third stands, head bowed, his posture allowing his left arm, which has no apparent hand, to be visible. This suggests a reference to the Spanish practice of amputating hands and feet from some Pueblo men who did not follow orders. In the middle ground, another Pueblo man is being whipped while the background contains the bodies of four men who have been hanged, their forms rendered in black.

To Conquer a Colossus carries the exaggerated graphic-novel style in a different direction. Here Garcia renders the Pueblo Revolt with a Pueblo man and woman battling much-larger armored Spanish forces. The central Pueblo man, with massively exaggerated muscles, holds a sword he must have captured from an enemy and has his other arm raised and holding an axe, ready to battle the five Spaniards in front of him. Another Spanish solder is behind him, ready to attack from his position. The roiling clouds Garcia has added to the composition emphasize the intensity of the battle.

Cochiti artist Diego Romero (b. 1964) is a potter who uses the interiors of his bowls and the exteriors of jars as canvases to paint images, both historic and contemporary. The arrival of the Spanish and the Pueblo Revolt have appeared as subjects various times. His style has similarities to that of Garcia as he, too, has been influenced by graphic novels.

But in many ways the contemporary artist whose work offers the closest comparison to Solomon's is Cochiti artist Virgil Ortiz (b. 1969). A multimedia

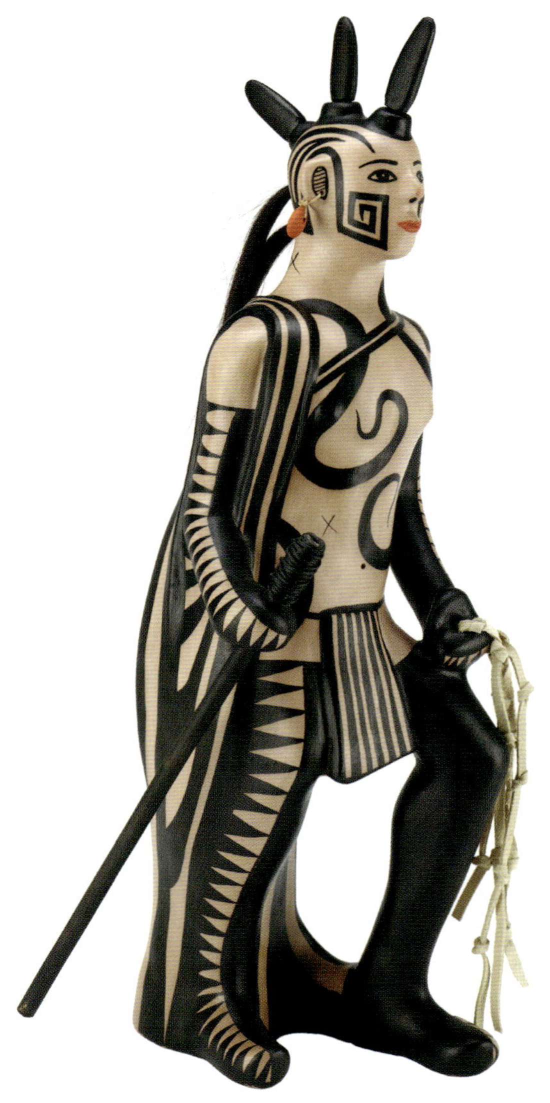

Figure 13. Virgil Ortiz, Cochiti Pueblo, *Po'pay*, 2012. Clay, paint, leather, and wood, 19 × 7 × 7 ½ in. Gift from Vicki and Kent Logan to the Collection of the Denver Art Museum, Denver, CO, 28.2014A-G. © Virgil Ortiz, courtesy of King Galleries. Image © Denver Art Museum.

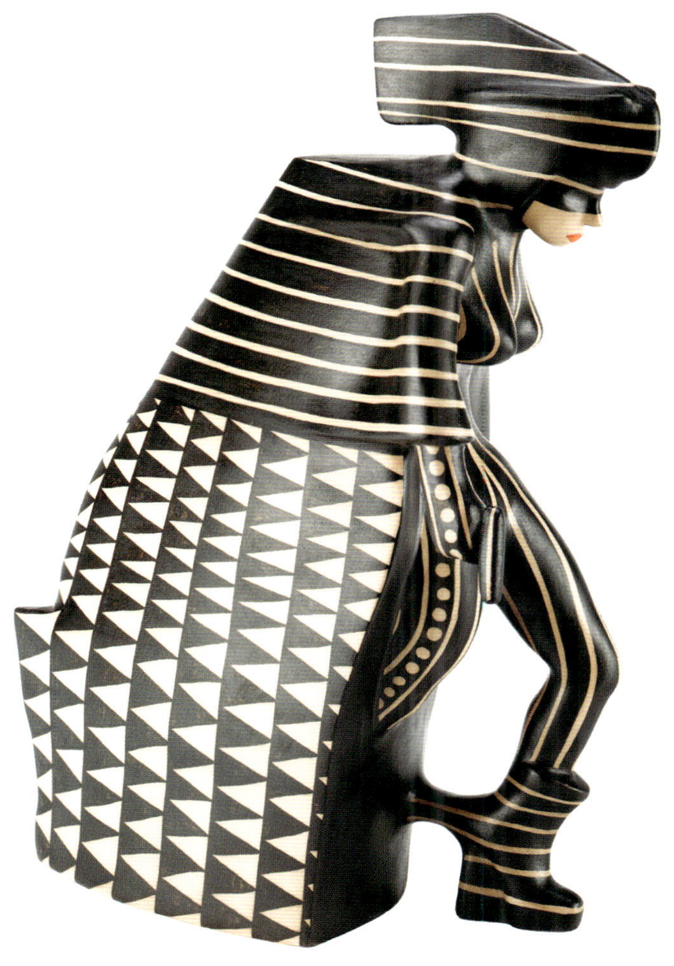

Figure 14. Virgil Ortiz, Cochiti Pueblo, Velocity Jar, 2012. Clay, slip, paint, 10 × 18 × 9 in. Gift from Vicki and Kent Logan to the Collection of the Denver Art Museum, Denver, CO, 2016.116. © Virgil Ortiz. Image © Denver Art Museum.

artist, Ortiz's ceramic sculptures, painted bowls, films, and videos address a history ranging from 1680 to 2180. His view is one of the past as well as of a contemporary revolt and a future one intended to keep history alive.

As he notes, he "was born with clay in his hands" and began making standing clay figures, rather than the seated storytellers for which Cochiti had become well known, when he was fifteen (Giago 2013). There had been a long, elaborate history of such standing figures, many satirical, in the later part of the nineteenth and early twentieth centuries, but because outsiders saw them both as idols and as vulgar, the tradition had died and was replaced by the more acceptable and extremely successful storytellers introduced by Cochiti ceramicist Helen Cordero (1915–1994) in 1964. Ortiz had begun making these when he was fourteen, but he quickly turned his attention to other types of figures (Giago 2013). He had never seen the nineteenth-century figures, some of which were up to three feet tall, until a collector showed the young potter his collection of them; Ortiz was amazed at the similarity (Giago 2013). "Without any guidance or having seen pictures of these earlier figures, mine looked exactly like them! My parents quickly took me outside and said in Keres [his Native language], 'we didn't teach you about or even show you any of these older figures. The clay has chosen you and is working through you to bring them back. Remember this moment. This is when you found out the clay is talking through you'" (King 2015, 17). He quickly expanded his own work and, as he traveled for exhibitions and saw the diverse ways in which people lived throughout the country, he adapted his work to include multiple tattoos and body piercings (Giago 2013).

He has said multiple times that his true goals are to keep Cochiti history alive and Cochiti youth interested in ceramics (Giago 2013; Batkin 1999, 32). His ceramics, videos, graphics, and fashion all draw on contemporary imagery. He has been particularly attentive to what visual effects attract younger members of his family when they watch movies, for example. Expanding his own visual language to incorporate what draws them in is one of his means of communicating effectively about Pueblo history (Giago 2013).

In 2007 Ortiz began his series of figurative forms that relate to the Pueblo Revolt. While grounded in history, he has used fictionalized characters to fill his narrative. He exhibited these as a group of Pueblo and Spanish figures prepared for combat facing each other across a chessboard during the 2010 "celebration" of Santa Fe's four hundredth anniversary (King 2015, 19). Figures like *Po'pay* from 2012 indicate his adherence to history, with the important leader carrying a knotted cord. But Ortiz also recognized his desire to push his narrative into the future while simultaneously connecting more securely with younger Pueblo people, particularly his nieces and nephews. Realizing their attraction to video games and other aspects of technology, he began to suggest exaggerated movement by the poses of his figures and the painted markings he applied to them. *Velocity* (2011) is a striking example. Parallel bands, angular forms, and bodies leaning forward into space all relay the action he sought. He has explored these ideas further in his videos and clothing as well.

In his recent work, Ortiz has carried the history of revolt not only into the present but into the future as well. *Revolt 1680/2180* continues the themes he had been investigating for a number of years, but it also includes the concepts of time travelers and lasers, for example—characters and weapons well-known from contemporary fiction. Ortiz's work is based in historical reality and the still-apparent effects of colonization, but he carries the idea of revolt well into the future.

Each of these artists has explored the arrival of the Spanish and the effects of their continuing efforts to convert or exterminate the people they encountered in the Southwest. While working in various styles and media, they have provided powerful works that are expressive as art intended to keep history alive. Floyd Solomon's etchings are a compelling part of these efforts.

CHAPTER 3

The Work of Floyd Solomon

Oral narratives within Native communities serve various purposes, one of the most important of which is to preserve history. Retelling episodes, both good and bad, ensures that subsequent generations are united to past actions and understand how the present came to be. Cultural values are transferred from one generation to the next as well, with these made even clearer through the past's connection to the present. For Native Americans and other colonized people, such narratives are, in a very basic way, acts of resistance. They subvert the never-ending effects of acculturation by proclaiming cultural identity and survival. Oral as well as visual and written narratives about the past, relayed from the culture's own point of view, loudly proclaim the continuing presence of people defying the absence that might otherwise be presumed.

Floyd Solomon, an artist of Laguna and Zuni heritage, grew up at Laguna Pueblo in New Mexico listening to his community's history as told by elders; these stories filled his life. At some other pueblos, narratives were not as inclusive. Simon Ortiz (b. 1941) has written that during his childhood at Acoma, a community all but destroyed at the end of the sixteenth century under orders from Don Juan de Oñate, governor general of northern New Spain, he heard no accounts of the vicious attack on the pueblo. "I've racked my memory trying to recall if there was any mention of it among many other stories told about 'the old days' of Acoma life, but, no, there were no oral stories about this terrible knowledge" (Ortiz 1999, 1). Ortiz argues for a complete knowledge of historical events so that Pueblo people can come to fully recognize themselves, their struggles, and their continuance (Ortiz

1999, 1). Although he heard stories of the dark events that came with the arrival of the Spanish, Floyd Solomon understood the need for Native people to have a more thorough understanding of the past.

As an artist, Solomon undertook a visual recounting of Pueblo history from his own knowledge of the past, an Indigenous knowledge positioned to reimagine history that is known largely from non-Native records. This was a personal knowledge that grew deeper and more comprehensive through his art. He effectively moved beyond the stereotypical accounts of the early confrontations with the Spanish, instead providing a more complete record of the destructive days from initial Spanish contact. He did not end there, however, as he continued his narrative into the mid-twentieth century with the never-ending interference of governmental bureaucracy and attempted assimilation. Solomon envisioned more than forty etchings in his account of Pueblo and European and Euro-American contact, but he was not able to complete the entire series. Twenty were finished, through the help of the Chamisa Foundation, and sadly those have not been widely viewed. Here, what he did accomplish and what he wanted to do beyond what remains can be more thoroughly understood.

Initially titled *Crucifixion of a Culture*, the stand that Solomon took in the etchings is clear. Blame for the barbaric actions against Pueblo people rests not just with soldiers and governmental officials but also, to a very large extent, with the Catholic Church and its representatives who, in Solomon's visual record, not only stand by while Pueblo people are murdered, maimed, and raped but also at times clearly direct actions against them and their cultural practices. Conversion of Native people, whether peacefully or by force, was at the heart of Spanish colonization of the Americas and was sanctioned by royal proclamation. But Solomon carries these ideas farther. The crucifixion portion of the title of his series relays not just conversion but destruction of human life and forced replacement of beliefs as well as a strong connection to the vital principles of Christianity. That this word should be central to Solomon's series underscores Pueblo attitudes toward their history and the colonialist actions they endured.

The title image for the series makes that combination clear. A vertically positioned cross includes the figure of the crucified Christ, but Solomon chose to present him with his head bent downward, his chin apparently touching his chest. A more frequent view of Christ presents him with his head slightly

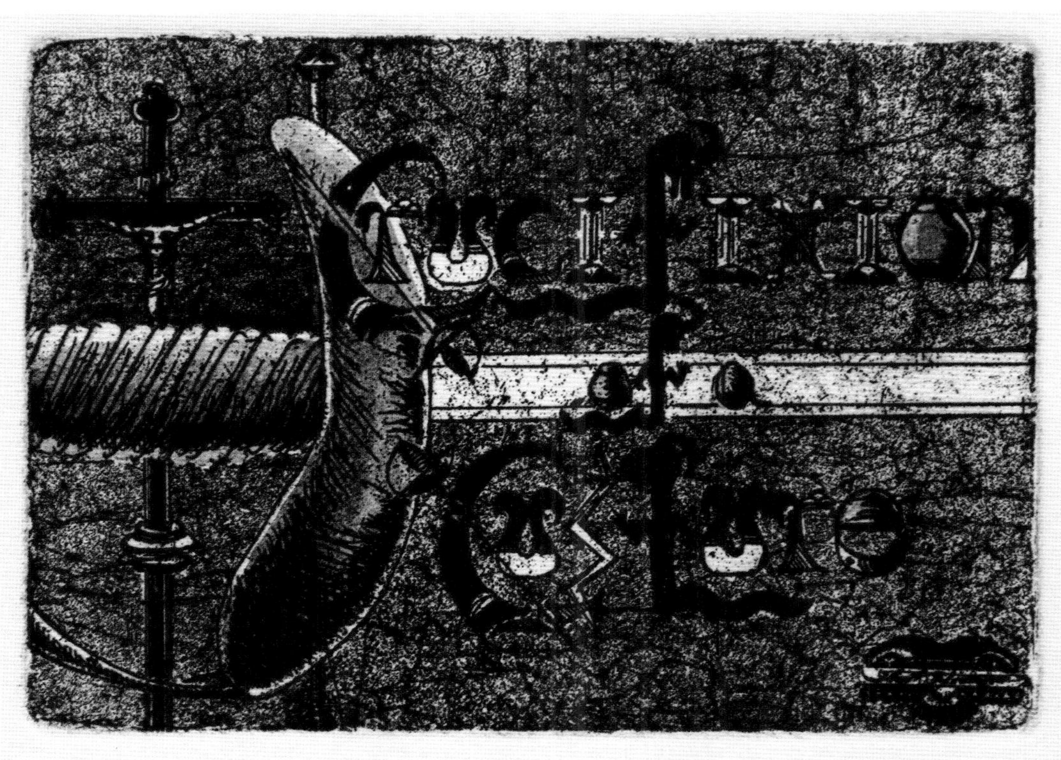

Figure 15. Floyd Solomon, *Crucifixion of a Culture,* undated. Etching, 4 1/16 × 5 3/4 in. Collection of Jeanne Solomon Bell. Image courtesy of Geistlight Photography, Albuquerque, NM.

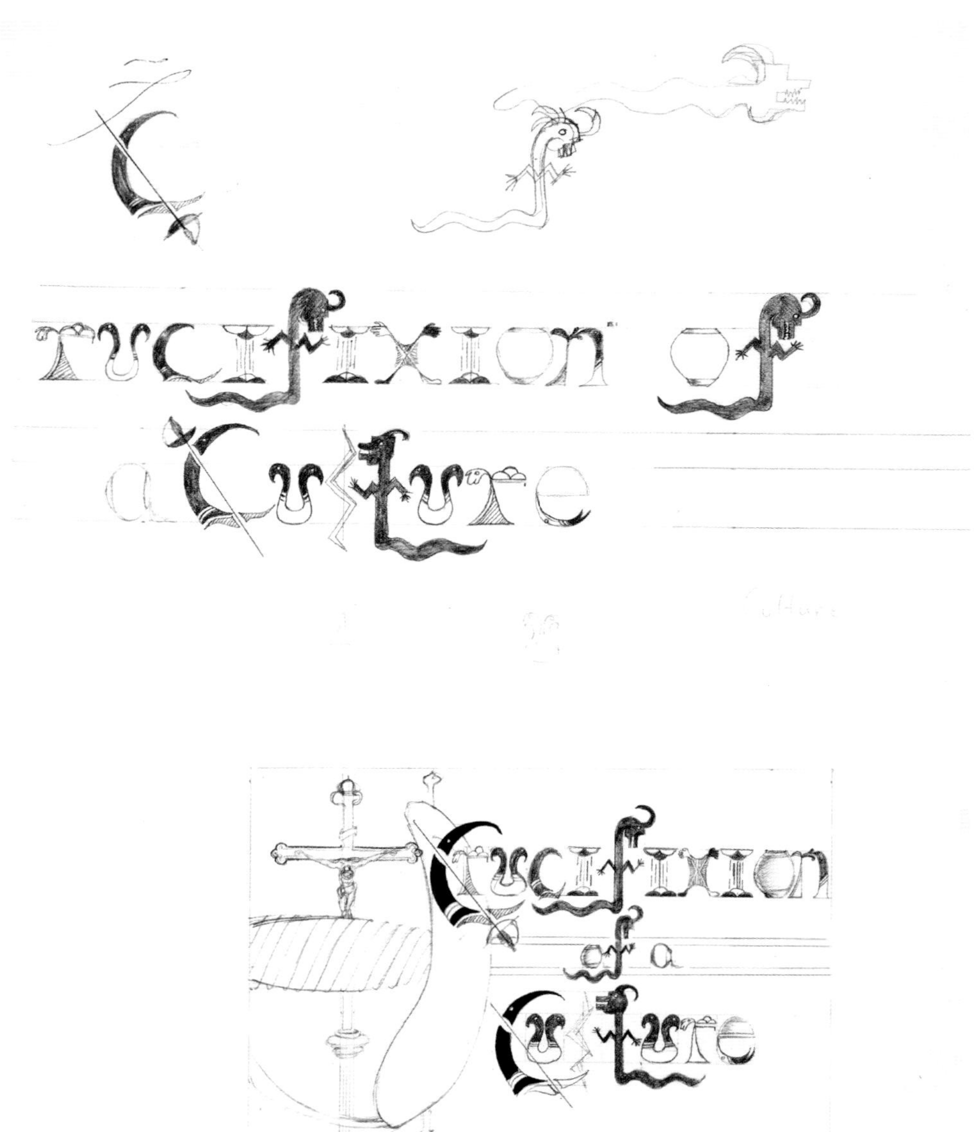

Figure 16. Floyd Solomon, sketches for title plate for *Crucifixion of a Culture*, undated. Collection of Jeanne Solomon Bell. Image courtesy of Geistlight Photography, Albuquerque, NM.

raised even in death, a sign of his victory and continuing life. Solomon's rendition suggests that a sorrowful Christ is horrified by what has been done to the Pueblo people in his name. More abstract but still apparent are the hilt and partial blade of the sword that cuts through the horizontal field of the drawing. Pueblo people are here as well, indicated by various symbols including rain clouds, horned serpents (or *awanyu*), and birds as well as other elements well-known from ceramic designs. With this initial image, Solomon set the stage for what was to follow: the violent clash of the Catholic Church, Spanish military forces, and Pueblo people.

Yet the Pueblo view of history is not the simple one of a people conquered, effectively enslaved, and nearly annihilated as the title might suggest. There are acts of resistance in Solomon's record, the most obvious being the Pueblo Revolt. He also included other ways in which Pueblo people maintained their heritage and their very being through the power of their spiritual beliefs and through strong human interactions. Indeed, Solomon wrote about how his prints and drawings linked him to the past, one he referred to as both violent and hidden (Solomon, Artist Statement). Revealing that hidden past inspired the entire *Crucifixion of a Culture* project.

After his service in the Navy and his studies at the University of New Mexico in accounting, he began his work as an artist for two simple but very personal reasons. First, he had begun to explore art as a diversion from his regular eight-hour per day job. From September 1982 to July 1986 he worked as a parent trainer specialist for the Education for Parents of Indian Children with the Special Needs Project in Bernalillo, New Mexico (Solomon, Curriculum Vitae). This was, by its very nature, an emotionally draining occupation. And second, he had also recently moved into a new home and needed something to hang on the walls (Solomon 1992b, 10).

Self-directed, Solomon initially developed the artistic techniques he employed by exploring libraries and bookstores. Many of his works were directly inspired by photographs as he developed an intensely realistic style. *Laguna Industry* (fig. 3), a charcoal-on-paper drawing from 1985, demonstrates the intensity with which he approached these renditions as well as his adherence to photographs. A turn-of-the-twentieth-century photograph of the Santa Fe Railroad line and Pueblo women bringing their pottery to sell to tourists on the incoming train inspired his charcoal drawing of the same subject. Solomon captured the details recorded in the photograph, including the women and their vessels, the machinery connected to the railroad stop, the train itself, and the landscape nearby. This is an important part of Laguna's history, one that the artist felt necessary to include in his overall visual record.

In 1989 Solomon left his full-time job to attend the IAIA in Santa Fe, where he took classes until 1991 to supplement his self-taught skills. He was concerned with learning the academic structure of the arts as well as developing a greater awareness of Native American art in order to understand how he might or might not fit within this category or "environment," as he referred to it (Solomon, "Biographical Information"). What he had read in books about artists had been almost exclusively about European and Euro-American ones; he found very little about Indigenous artists. Many issues needed to be explored through the Native voice, and he could not understand why they had not been (Solomon, Commentary in Sketchbook). However, he became more fully aware of how the market directed and controlled Native American art through his experiences at IAIA. He was also concerned about renditions of ritual subjects to fulfill the desires of the market. "Through a juxtaposition of Indian and European art I have understood the extent tourism has controlled the direction of modern Indian art. The mainstream economy has determined the iconography currently being used in traditional and contemporary Indian art. This has created conflict among Indian communities and artists due to the rampant exploitation of religious concepts and imagery for money" (Solomon, "Biographical Information"). He was particularly offended by contemporary reproductions of objects based on the ritual lives of Native communities. Solomon referred to much of contemporary Native American art, both these types of reproductions and many other art forms, as "trading post art" (Solomon, Commentary in Sketchbook). He was troubled by a continuation of a style of painting developed in the 1930s in Santa Fe, the so-called Studio style given its affiliation with instructor Dorothy Dunn's studio at the Santa Fe Indian School. The style, with figures crisply outlined and filled with flat applications of opaque watercolor and sometimes referred at as the flat style, has generally been used to depict genre and dance scenes, often showing no impact of the changes brought with the passage of time, as if Native people were frozen in a romanticized past.

Solomon worked in two extremely different ways, however each was historically oriented. One was closer to the commercially successful style of the Santa Fe art world and was connected to the intense realism he explored in *Laguna Industry*. In large oil paintings, he often focused on single figures rendered with very detailed clothing and sometimes ceramic vessels, frequently set against the dark-black background of the canvas. The lifelike images seem to jump from the picture plane and enter the viewer's space. As he noted, "I paint Laguna people in a traditional Renaissance fashion because I believe, when Indians paint themselves flat, it's a condition of their mind—that's how they see themselves. I'm trying to influence how they think about themselves by making them, perceivably, three-dimensional. I believe, by doing this, they will gain a greater appreciation of their contemporary selves" (Solomon 1998). His concern about the flat style of painting or the Studio style and its effects on Native people—how it encouraged them to see themselves as something not fully dimensional, not completely developed—echoes concerns Simon Ortiz expressed about the lack of knowledge Native people have about their own past in the present. Solomon also used this three-dimensional approach "to develop a means of historically documenting what is currently being lost by American Indians . . . making foods, unique social interaction, reflecting the subtlety of social change" (Solomon 1992a). This painting style was clearly readable and could be readily understood by both Native and non-Native viewers given their familiarity with it; he referred to his large paintings as being "like public speeches" (Solomon, Statement for the Wheelwright Museum). These paintings, he observed, also allowed him "to survive monetarily" (Solomon 1992a); such paintings were what was expected by many purchasers.

The prints that comprise *Crucifixion of a Culture* as well as various other etchings he created are not in the style he used in his oil paintings, nor do they serve the same purpose. He discussed these prints as an art of social criticism (Solomon 1992a). He credited Ada Medina, from whom he took drawing courses at the IAIA, with encouraging him to alter the direction of his art. Her methods required that the students with whom she worked dig deep within themselves to express important concerns in their respective art forms.

> This process began the reassessment of my social programming and

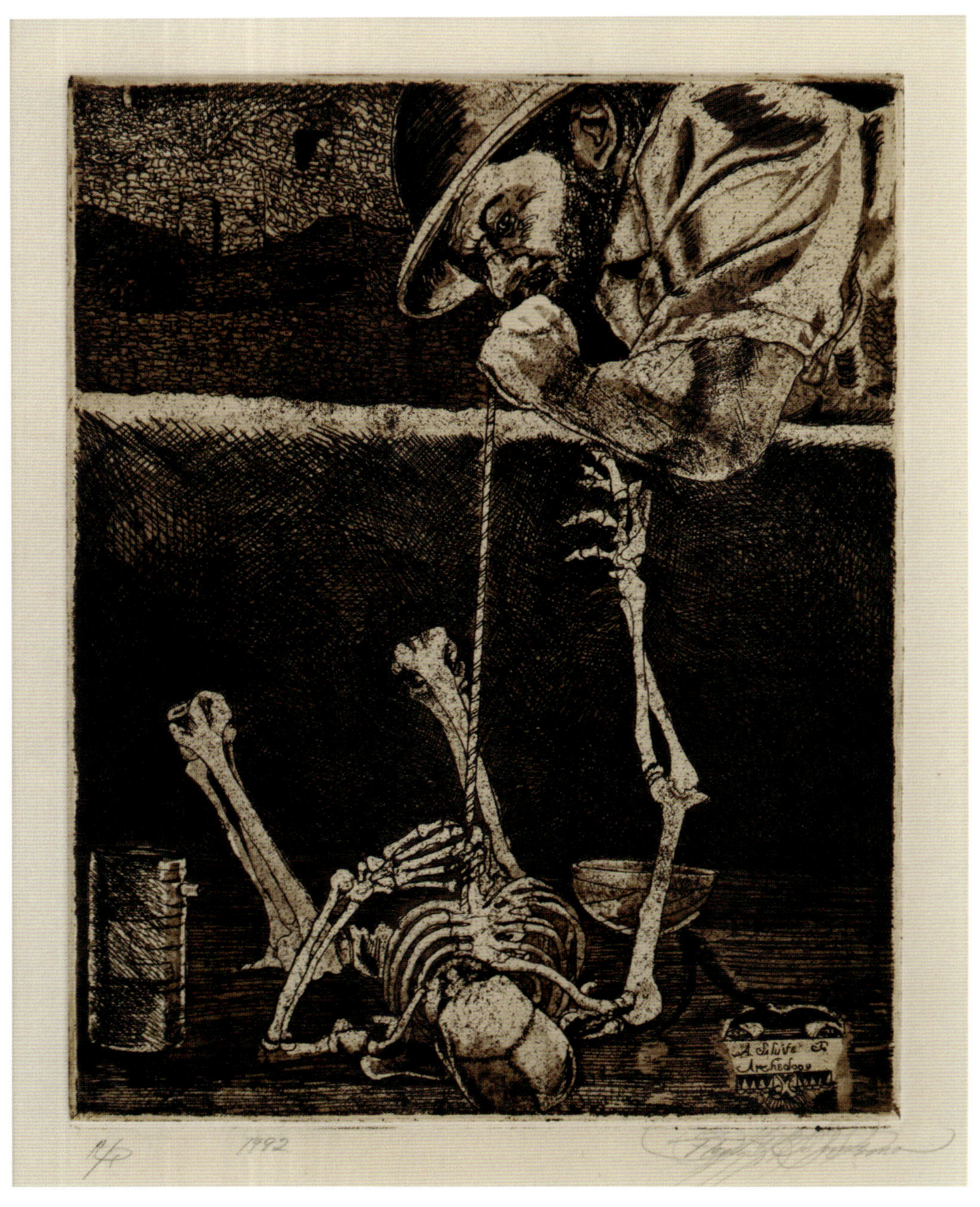

Figure 17. Floyd Solomon, *A Salute to Archaeology*, undated. Etching, 9 ⅜ × 7 ⅜ in. Collection of Jeanne Solomon Bell. Image courtesy of Geistlight Photography, Albuquerque, NM.

> seeking unexplored territories of American Indian art. I have been hard pressed to research historical events objectively and superimpose an Indian perspective, however research has directed me toward understanding the broader application of art as a communication instrument.
>
> My objectives include seeing past current institutionalized academia and attempting to understand the impact of the bombardment of European philosophy on American Indians. (Solomon 1992a)

Solomon was concerned that many Native artists were funneled into the arts because they did not perform well in academic settings and that this led to an assumption that these artists would not have to be able to speak about their art, defend it, and be innovative (Solomon 1998, 36). As a member of a conservative community, Solomon was also troubled about the place of individual rights and their regulation. "At what level does this affect the expression of Indian artists? How are we learning to exercise our freedom of speech, and how does that affect our freedom of expression, particularly in our new art forms?" (Solomon 1998, 35). In exploring the past from a Native point of view, a past he referred to as dark and hidden, Solomon demonstrated his dedication to ensuring that the stories he heard as a child would be passed on to many others, both Native and non-Native, in clear, effective ways.

His etching *A Salute to Archaeology* of 1992 was not part of the *Crucifixion of a Culture* series. It does, however, offer a view of his critical stance on the way his people have been and continue to be treated. The archaeologist leans over a grave, having tied a rope to the skeleton below, and prepares to remove the ancient remains from their previously undisturbed resting place. A ceramic bowl had been placed with the human remains and this, too, will come into the archaeologist's hands, for nothing, it seems, remains untouched. The colonization that the artist explored in the prints depicting actions from the late sixteenth and seventeenth centuries has continued with new violations of freedom and disruptions of sacred practices.

Solomon essentially taught himself the techniques of intaglio printmaking. Etching and aquatint were the most effective tools for the emotions that he wanted to fill his images, his language for his purposes (Solomon, Artist Statement). In this he followed Francisco Goya's successful use of the medium in

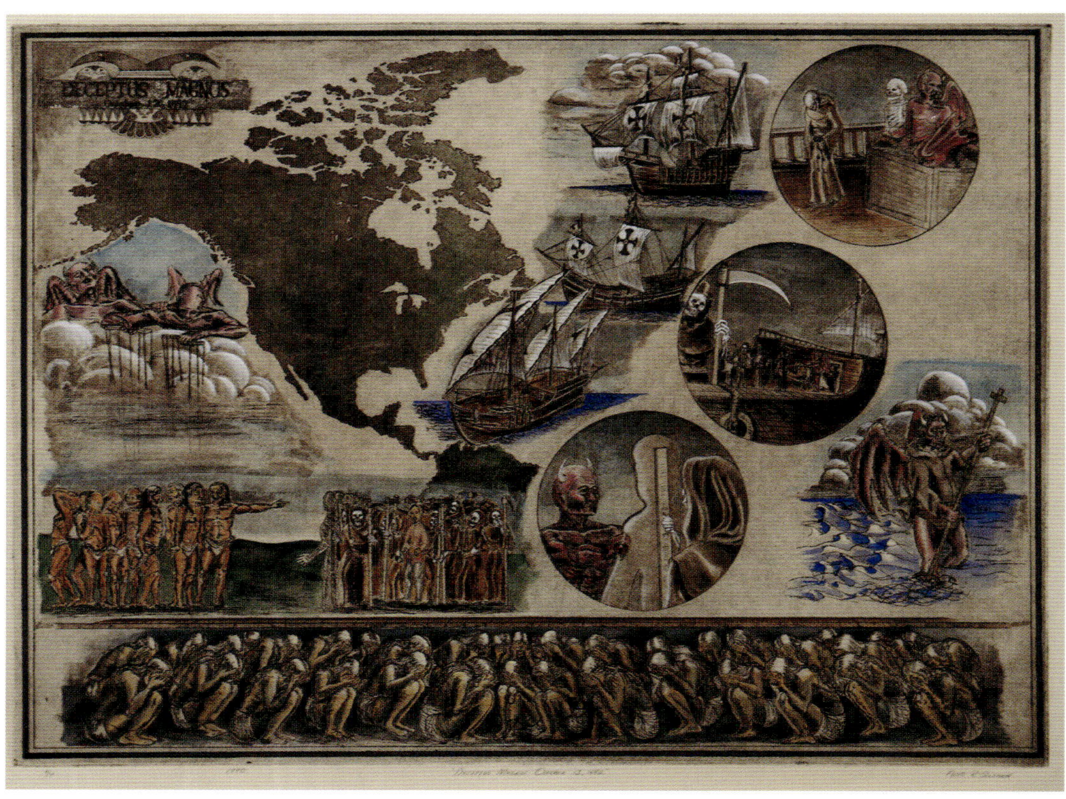

Figure 18. Floyd Solomon, *Deceptus Magnus—October 12, 1492*, 1990. Etching, 22 × 30 in. University of New Mexico Art Museum, Albuquerque, NM, 2017.2.1. Image courtesy of Geistlight photography, Albuquerque, NM.

his series *Disasters of War*. Other artists who, like Goya, worked both as painters and as printmakers were also inspirational to Solomon. He often spoke about the power of light in Rembrandt's work, for example (Bell 2012).

Various figurative forms included in the artist's 1992 large, ambitious 27 ½ × 23 ½ inch etching *Deceptus Magnus—October 12, 1492* appear in the *Crucifixion of a Culture* prints. There are, however, great differences between *Deceptus Magnus* and the series. While each of the approximately 5 × 7 inch prints from *Crucifixion of a Culture* is almost exclusively focused on one incident and related actions, the larger print pulls together various subsets. Three roundels contain devil and skeletal images, and the lower right corner echoes this theme. Ships bringing the Spanish to the Americas dominate a central diagonal line, and puppeteers control actions below them to the left portion of the picture frame. Segmented from the main body of the print is a lower horizontal section arranged like a predella panel in a Renaissance painting. Here figures crouch, huddling as if to somehow avoid the fate that awaits them above.

As the date in the title suggests, this large etching is an exploration of the idea of Columbus and the arrival of Europeans. *Deceptus Magnus* was the artist's way of expressing what he termed the big deception. It did not matter to Solomon whether this was correct Latin or not; it only mattered that the title relayed his intent. Three ships in the mid-section of the composition appear to move from right to left and carry Columbus and his men to the Americas; North and Central America and the upper portion of South America are all visible while Europe is an assumed reality. The right-to-left movement is not here simply because that direction reflects the Eurocentric view of the land that awaited Columbus. Solomon observed that he chose this direction to organize the large print because it is contrary to standard left-to-right Western reading systems (Solomon 1992b).

Skeletons and devils fill the composition. Images of skeletons, of course, have a logical connection to death and were well established in European manuscript illustration by the Middle Ages. German artists, in particular, often used such skeletal representations to suggest death in the sixteenth century. Painters and printmakers like Hans Holbein and Albrecht Durer are among the prominent artists whose work Solomon undoubtedly knew. Holbein's *Dance of Death* woodcuts are, in particular, strong potential models for Solomon to have examined. Such skeletal images that engaged with people of various classes and in differing activities focus on the universal, unrelenting destruction of death. In *Deceptus Magnus* and in many of his other etchings and drawings, Solomon relied upon this readily understandable figure to emphasize the destruction of so many Native lives. The entirety of *Deceptus Magnus* is not only a response to the 1992 quincentennial of Columbus's arrival in the Americas, with its great celebrations by non-aboriginal people, but also a condemnation of what transpired with the advent of Europeans, especially evil, disease, and death.

Drawings from Solomon's sketchbooks provide clues to the inspiration for some of the imagery here. A winged figure carrying a trident surmounted by a cross appears in the lower right corner of *Deceptus Magnus* and is most certainly Satan with an added reference to the Church. A fully detailed drawing of this figure appears among Solomon's sketches. A piece of writing next to the figure in his sketchbook notes, "Christopher Columbus, Resource National Geographic November, 1975" (Solomon, Commentary in Sketchbook). That issue of *National Geographic Magazine* included an article unfortunately entitled "Christopher Columbus, The Sailor Who Gave Us the New World" (Scofield 1975). Several words in that relatively brief title must have infuriated the artist. Who is the "us" to whom Columbus "gave" something that was neither his nor anyone else's to give? Even "New World" carries regrettable overtones.

The specific resource to which Floyd Solomon referred in his sketchbook is the appearance in the article on Columbus of five images purported to be portraits of the explorer (Scofield 1975, 618–19). None were made during Columbus's lifetime, so his true appearance remains unknown. However, of the five, Solomon chose a woodcut by the sixteenth-century Swiss artist Tobias Stimmer as the model for his figure of Columbus as Satan. The same cast of the man's eyes, his head partially turned to his right, the angular treatment of his cheekbones, and his broad forehead appear in both Stimmer's and Solomon's images. Solomon used this portrait as the basis for his representation of Satan in *Deceptus Magnus*.

Solomon placed symbols of his own clans, eagle and water, in the upper-left corner of the picture plane as integral parts of the print's title. In an August 1992 interview with Nancy Mithlo, Solomon offered an in-depth analysis of the complex symbolism found in *Deceptus Magnus*.

Non-Native figures in the print are connected to evil in various ways. In the lower-right corner, Columbus as Satan uses his trident with cross to stir or create "the sea of turmoil" (Solomon 1992b, 13). Satan appears again in the three roundels that angle diagonally from right to left in the right portion of the print. Solomon rendered the "devil, which is evil in its purest form . . . giving this European the symbol of death and disease . . . a cloak in which to hide his body. To me, that's the cloak of religion" (Solomon 1992b, 12). An image of death appears aboard a ship in the second roundel, not only cloaked in the garment in which he appears in the initial rendering but also carrying a scythe and shackles. "The scythe is to harvest people, the shackles is to enslave them" (Solomon 1992b, 12). Then the devil stands facing death, but between them is a flat human form. This is another tool given to the cloaked figure, "a cardboard cutout of a human being, which to me symbolizes the mockery of humanity . . . of humanism that Europeans display. So how they use this, then, is when they breed the Indians, you see these cloaked skeletal figures kind of . . . making a mockery of humanity" (Solomon 1992b, 13). Thus, the devil has presented death with his responsibilities.

To the left of the final roundel, a group of skeletal images stand with their cardboard cutouts facing a group of Native people who are warning each other about the true nature of these flat images of humanity. However, Solomon also included a chief who "is a puppet" as indicated by the devil in the clouds above controlling the strings of a puppeteer. The chief

> poses himself as a puppet of evil, and since he's being controlled by evil, he welcomes death and disease upon his people. And the next two figures are talking about war. But all they have is a bow with no arrows, so basically they're defenseless. The next figure is an old man, the symbol of wisdom. One of the old men is also being controlled by the devil, and being that he is controlled, he is causing more confusion among the so-called elders of their time . . . their conveyance of wisdom . . . becomes confused. The last two figures on the left are two younger men who are walking away in frustration and to me that symbolizes the divisiveness of Indians even in . . . contemporary [times]. (Solomon 1992b, 12)

Below the main body of the print, the mass of crouching figures appear and are presented as if they are under the deck of the ship. These are women referred to by Solomon as

> the weeping widows . . . who weep because many of these women . . . they came and began to be subject to the slaughter by the Europeans. . . . they had killed many of their own families, merely to survive . . . or not to allow their families to be subject to the torture that was being conducted by Columbus and his men. . . . And they're weeping also because in one part, they see the past and the future of Indians. They see the gradual disintegration of belief, of traditionalism, and so in a sense they are weeping for the future. (Solomon 1992b, 13)

Solomon also carried this interpretation into the present with the small number of Native people who remained after Columbus's arrival and subsequent violence.

Deceptus Magnus is certainly filled with the social criticism about which Solomon spoke. One clear example is the figure of Columbus as Satan stirring the waters with his trident and surmounted by a cross in the lower-right corner of the large print. Here Solomon has commented on the duality of the Church, but he is also citing the creation of a sea of turmoil. This is a biblical reference to chaos in the world, a chaos that Solomon felt began at the time of European contact (Solomon 1992b, 13–14). It was European contact that altered relationships of people with the world and with each other. Other Native as well as some non-Native people to whom he showed this image and with whom he discussed its symbolism agreed enthusiastically that "this is something that we have always felt, but have never been able to express" (Solomon 1992b, 14).

In his historically based works filled with social criticism, which he differentiated from the works documenting what he felt was being currently lost in Native cultures, Solomon also relied upon European and Euro-American approaches to rendering figures and relaying narratives. These approaches included foreshortening, linear perspective, and three-dimensional modeling, and they were, he felt, clear and readily understood by a wider audience. He wanted to share what he knew about the past with both Native and non-Native people (Solomon, Artist Statement). His art also employs the vocabulary of the colonizers in ways that reconfigure it to meet his ends.

He was definitely inspired by European masters, but he turned the works around, as it were, and created solid evidence of survival, of Pueblo people actively renewing their culture despite the attempted genocide they endured. Like many Native writers and artists, he sometimes employed irony or black humor. These are difficult subjects, and irony and parody not only make the impact of images and stories stronger, they also reflect more efficiently the Native narrative approach. Gerald Vizenor, among others, has written eloquently about the importance of continuing narratives of Native people as survivance; these ideas apply equally to Solomon's visual narratives. Vizenor sees that "Native survivance stories are renunciations of dominance, tragedy, and victimry" (Vizenor 1999, vii). Solomon considered art another kind of voice: "Despite all the historical issues related to oppression of the native culture, it is important to me to continue seeking a way or language in visual art to say what I feel inside" (Solomon, Commentary in Sketchbook). His retellings of the events that comprise his print series, although the incidents are tragic and barbaric, are clear evidence that the conquerors did not succeed; the Pueblo people remain.

At times, Solomon used his sketchbooks as journals, writing about his feelings, concerns, and influences. When he was forty-nine, he mused about the lack of writing by Native artists about their own art. He had been reading *Artists on Art*, a volume edited by Robert Goldwater and Marco Treves, which included thoughts about art by artists from the thirteenth to the twentieth centuries; these were, of course, European and, in the nineteenth and twentieth centuries, Euro-American artists recording their remarks on and analyses of various art forms (Goldwater and Treves 1975). Many of the artists documented their reasons for creating art and what its value was. In addition to the obvious Eurocentric nature of the accounts and the choices made by the editors, Solomon was concerned that Native artists had recorded nothing similar; they had left "very little information behind as a means of guiding other native artists" (Solomon, Commentary in Sketchbook). He continues, "I have often wondered if this phoneme [*sic*] is related to the oral traditions of native people, the psychological oppression imposed upon native people by 'white society' and its institutions. Whether the native artist actually felt confident enough to have left written matter behind (for which he or she would eventually be evaluated) or whether the person was just plain lazy" (Solomon,

Commentary in Sketchbook). In either case, he hoped that his own written accounts would "one day help another 'native artist' or shed light on a facet of Indian art" (Solomon, Commentary in Sketchbook).

Both Solomon's sketchbooks and the etchings are filled with forms reminiscent of various European and American masters. He was particularly affected by Francisco Goya (1746–1828), Käthe Kollwitz (1867–1945), and Rembrandt (1606–1669) (Solomon, Artist Statement). Each of these European masters is a prominent printmaker, while both Goya and Rembrandt are also well-known painters. Both Goya and Kollwitz developed themes of war reflective of the times and locations in which they lived. Theirs are more contemporary views and commentaries on life around them or recent memories while Solomon's is, of course, a visual record of the past inspired by oral accounts continuing into the present. Rembrandt, by contrast, was not an artist who generally focused on such violent images. He was, simply put, a master printmaker whose etchings are more spiritually and psychologically focused. Solomon would have readily identified with the cruelty and suffering reflected in Goya's and Kollowitz's works in his desire to relay the story of Spanish contact, the Pueblo Revolt, and the subsequent imposition of rules and regulations meant to suppress Native lifeways, but he was also drawn to the power of Rembrandt's images.

Goya's works, especially *Disasters of War*—his series of eighty-two etchings created between 1810 and 1820—are, in many ways, the closest in character to *Crucifixion of a Culture* given the similar conception of a series of images and the explicit manner in which he rendered war not as a romantic or heroic action but as inhumane and brutal. Kollwitz also created cycles of prints and explored the effects of war. Her two series *The Weavers* and *Peasant War* are both concerned with the realities and impact of war. She, too, provided explicit views, often emphasizing emotional turmoil that she suggests through one or two figures rather than the larger number of figures Goya frequently represented. Solomon used both of these approaches in his work to more fully detail the effects of Spanish cruelty.

Each of these European masters of printmaking was an artist whose works were well known to Solomon, as were their predecessors in earlier centuries. Floyd Solomon was a man working in the latter part of the twentieth century and, while he had studied business and accounting during his years at the

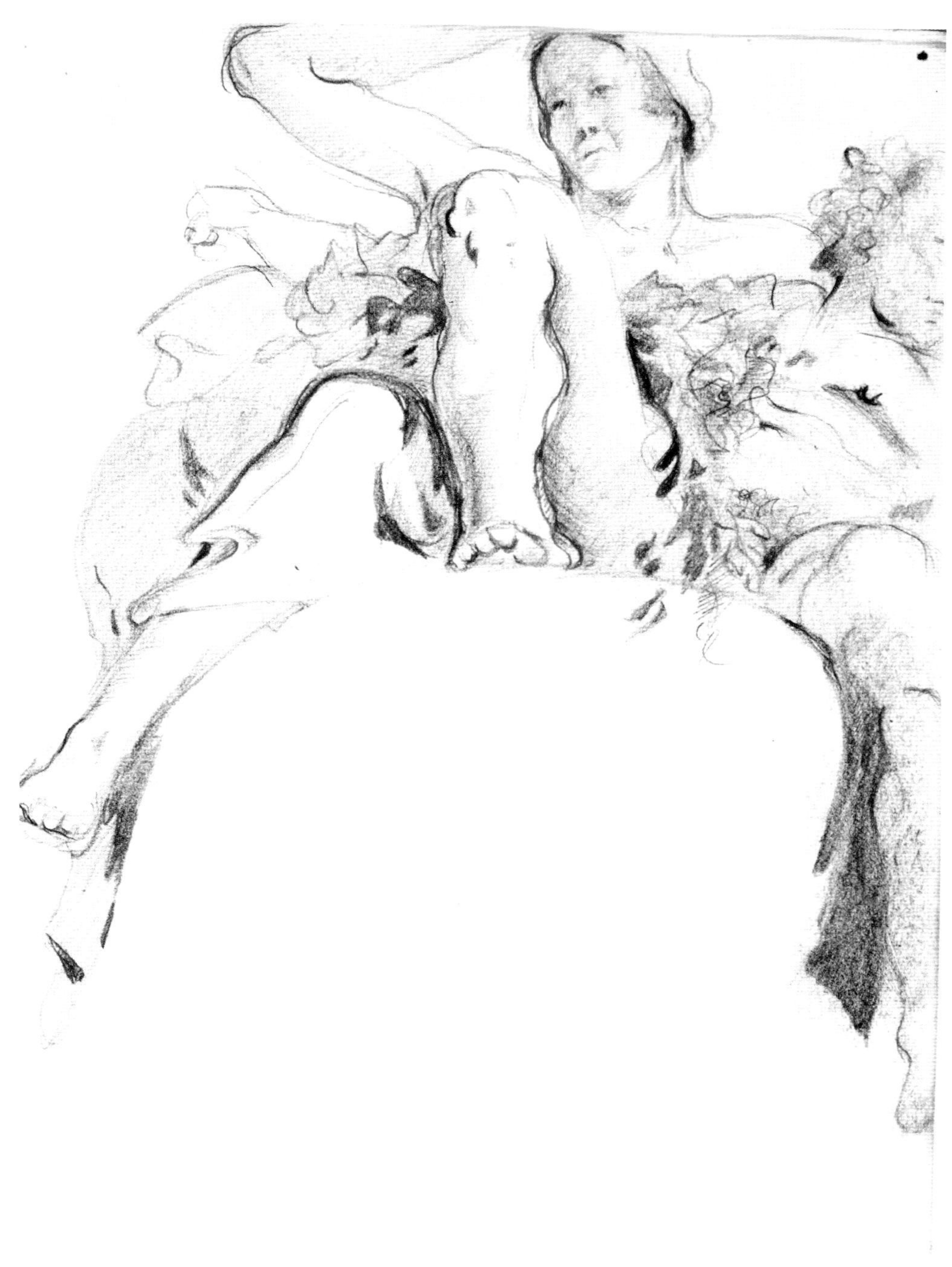

Figure 19. Floyd Solomon, Untitled Sketch, undated. Collection of Jeanne Solomon Bell. Image courtesy of Geistlight Photography, Albuquerque. NM.

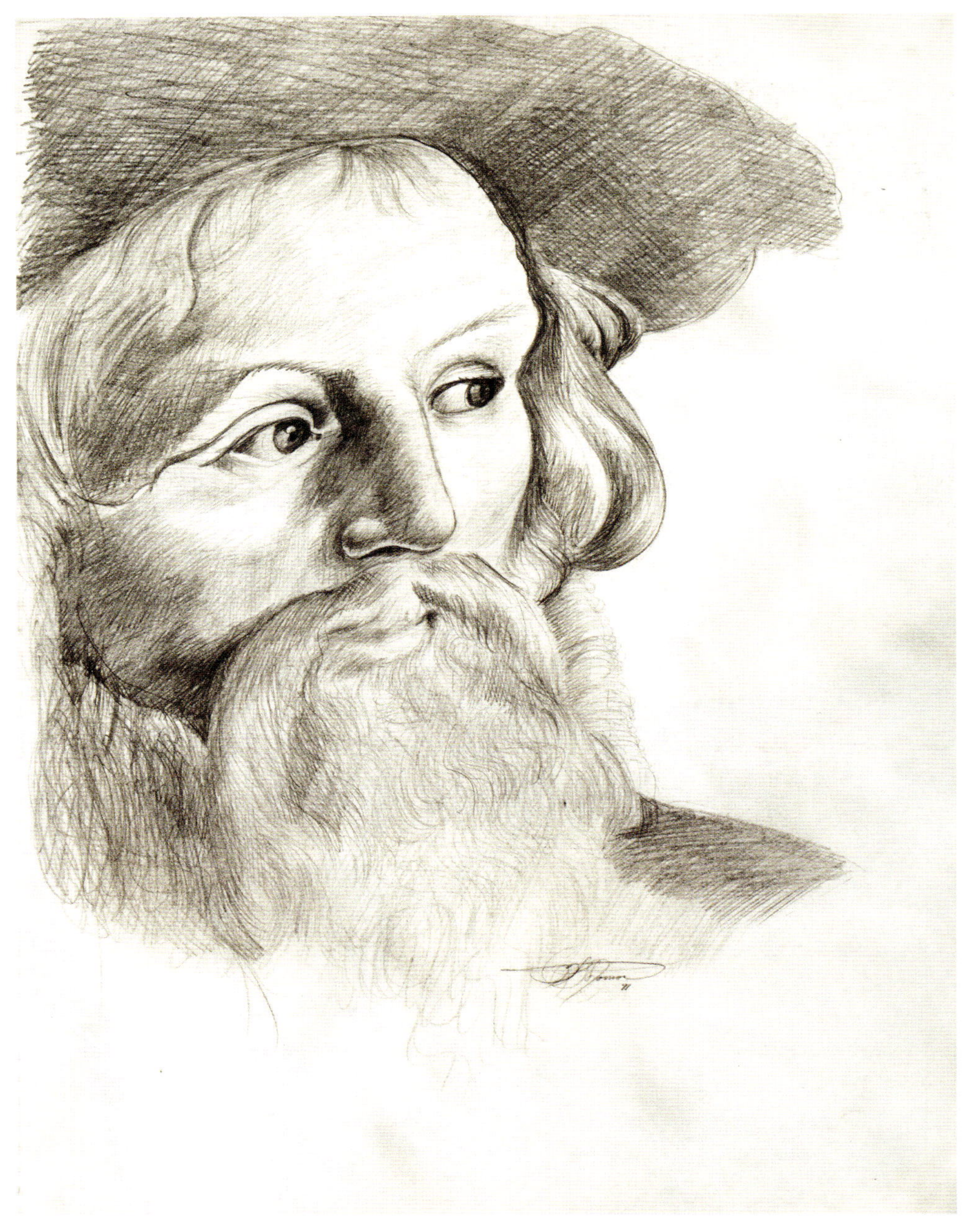

Figure 20. Floyd Solomon, *Untitled Sketch*, undated. Collection of Jeanne Solomon Bell. Image courtesy of Geistlight Photography, Albuquerque, NM.

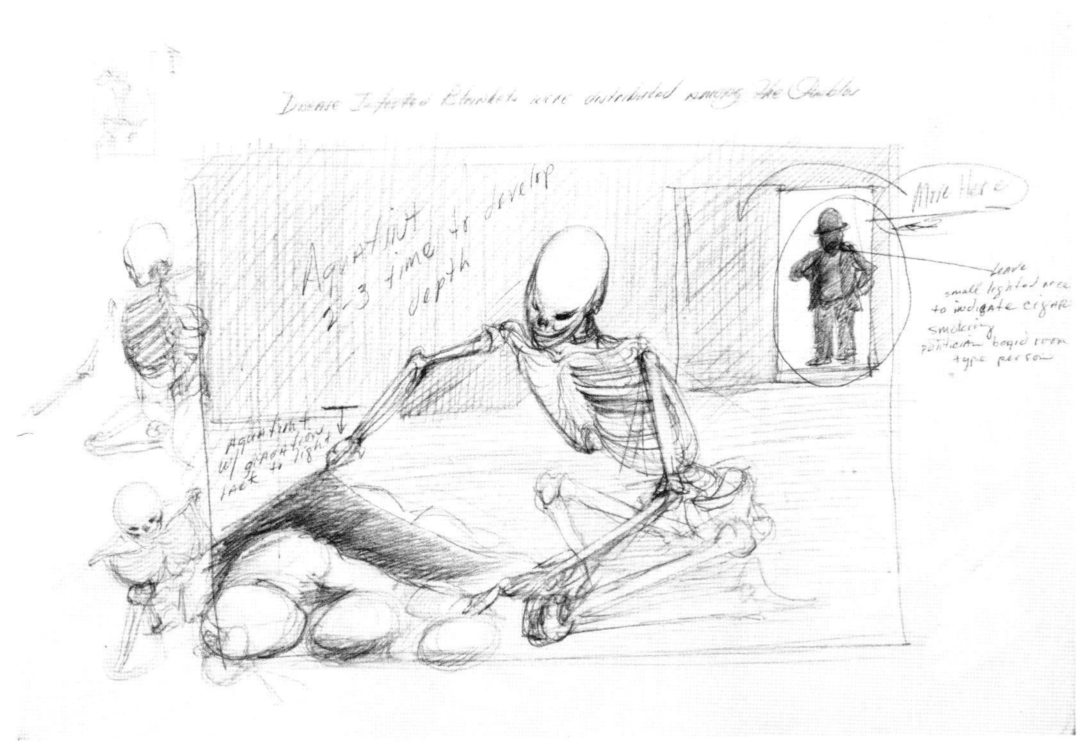

Figure 21. Floyd Solomon, *Untitled Sketch*, undated. Collection of Jeanne Solomon Bell. Image courtesy of Geistlight Photography, Albuquerque, NM.

University of New Mexico, he attended the IAIA closer to the time he was working on the etchings. Libraries and bookstores were also avenues to wider knowledge of the arts. Therefore, his knowledge of the history of art was extensive. He admired the work of various artists whose draughtsmanship and narrative power relayed the kind of messages he sought to impart, whether or not their subjects were war and colonialism. He drew upon many influences to tell his stories in the ways he wanted.

Solomon's sketchbooks include various studies for portions of individual prints. While occasionally full sketches for a complete scene were blocked out on the page, single or small groups of figures dominate as he was determining poses and expressions he would subsequently combine into completed compositions. Various positions for Spanish soldiers are presented here, some with the men on horseback and others focusing only on the soldiers' heads and helmets. Figure studies of a very conventional nature are also here, with nude figures indicating his ability to render the human form. Other figures are obvious references to Michelangelo, for example, with the hand of God reaching toward that of Adam to bestow life on the first man. Sketches like these are not full compositions but rather focus on portions of the works of great masters of interest to Solomon. It was the power of that gesture that he captured in his rendition. Additional notes contained in the books discuss other masters such as Giotto (d. 1337). Some of the most fully realized drawings reference Caravaggio (1571–1610), including a Bacchus figure with a container of fruit. An additional delicately rendered bearded man who wears a soft-brimmed hat and looks to his left is the figure generally taken to be Saint Matthew from Caravaggio's *The Calling of St. Matthew* (1599–1600). Here Solomon has been intrigued by the appearance of the tax collector looking toward the pointing finger of Christ, who summons him, demanding that he give up the life of luxury in which he is shown engaged in the complete Baroque painting. Another screaming head is based on a portion of Leonardo da Vinci's now lost *The Battle of Anghiari* (1505).

Yet Solomon was also intrigued by more contemporary artists. Drawings in his sketchbooks are variations on early twentieth-century Cubism, and one startlingly complex fully realized drawing suggests his knowledge of Escher (1898–1972) as it combines multiple viewpoints of a Pueblo with three kivas seen from above as well as parallel to the groundline.

Less detailed sketches suggest subjects of Pueblo history that the artist intended to explore. Some of these would undoubtedly have been part of the larger *Crucifixion of a Culture* series. One extremely powerful group of sketches, with handwritten notations suggesting a title—"Disease Infected Blankets Were Distributed among the Pueblos"—references one of the means by which diseases were transmitted to Native people who had no immunity to them.

Inside a room, a skeletal image of death wraps three sleeping figures—one of them larger than the others, suggesting two children and their mother—in such a blanket. A small, non-Native man dressed in trousers, a short jacket, and a hat stands smoking in the distant doorway beyond the interior scene. Two other sketches of skeletons appear on the margins of the blocked-off larger composition. While never completed, the sketches are a clear indication of the strength that a final etching would have had.

Solomon's sketchbooks are those of someone attempting to understand the methods of previous artists and working through ideas to reach the best possible solution to present an essential narrative. He was simultaneously honing his representational skills and learning the technique of etching. Notes appear that offer specific information about the process itself, including adjusting the amount of time the plate should be immersed in the acid bath, for example.

Through his experimentation with different styles and close examination of the works of other artists, Floyd Solomon learned his art as most other artists before him and since have done. He was not someone merely absorbing influences but was, rather, an artist intent on telling the stories he felt vital in the most effective manner possible. To that end, he altered his style in various drawings or in different parts of his series to reflect the points he needed to emphasize. In some cases, he changed the style to reflect the time period of the action involved. Solomon used approaches from previous centuries and masters to bring his narrative of European contact into the present. This is not a nostalgic use of form. Rather, it creates, from these multiple influences, a space in which powerful communication can occur. He was an early and effective proponent of the reclamation of Pueblo history as a vital strategy in contemporary Native American life and art. In his own words, "Sharing this painful part of my history has helped me work through the agony of

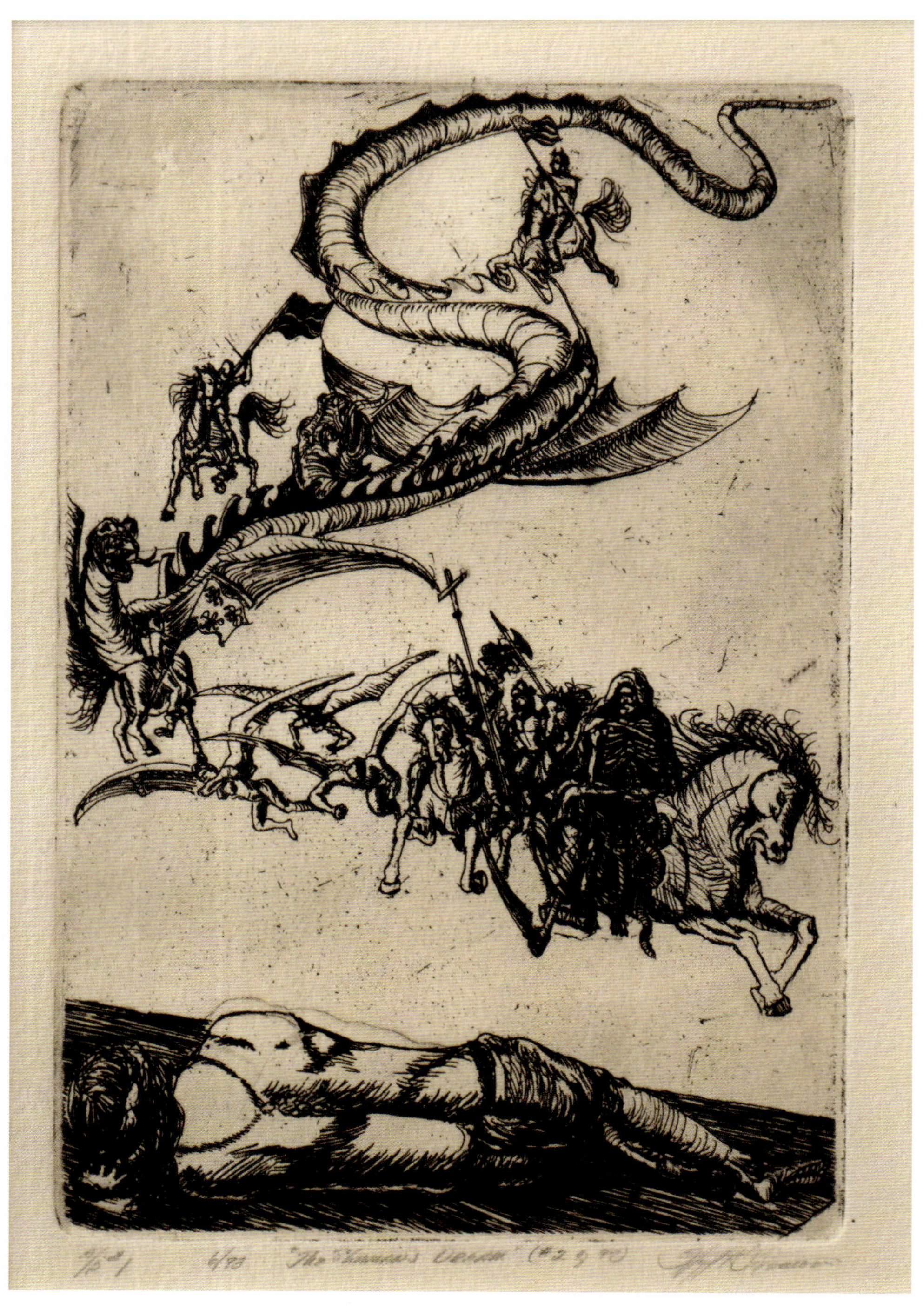

Figure 22. Floyd Solomon, *The Shaman's Dream*, undated. Etching. 7 5⁄16 × 4 7⁄8 in. Collection of Jeanne Solomon Bell. Image courtesy of Geistlight Photography, Albuquerque, NM.

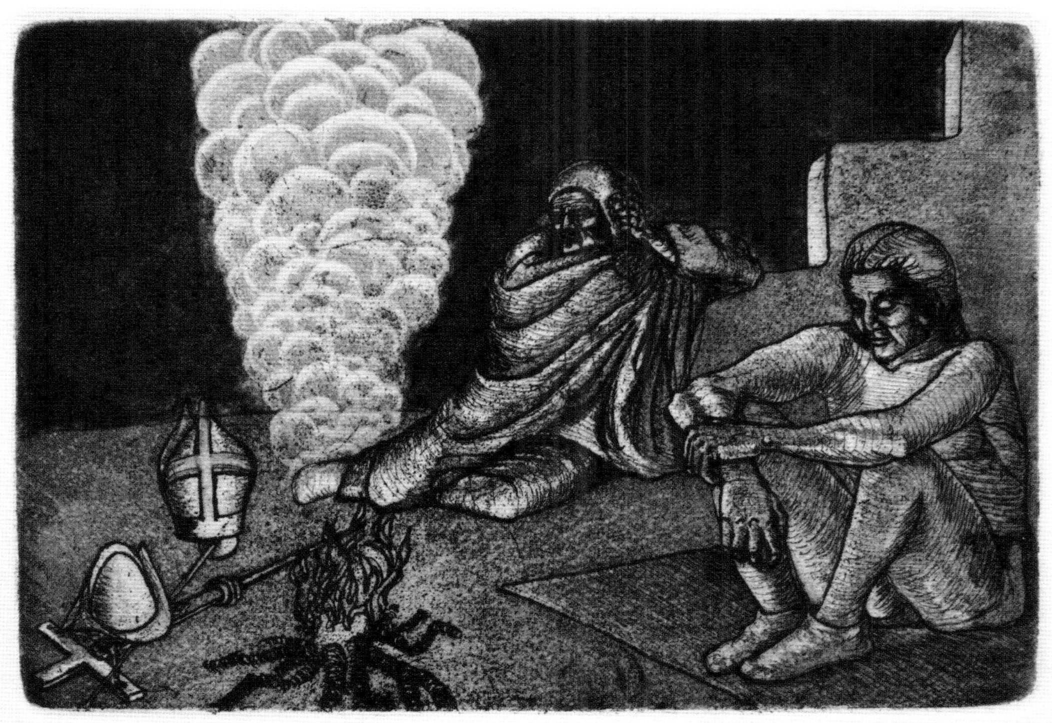

Figure 23. Floyd Solomon, *Contemplating Visual Symbols,* undated. Etching, 4 ¾ × 6 ⅞ in. Collection of Jeanne Solomon Bell. Image courtesy of Geistlight Photography, Albuquerque, NM.

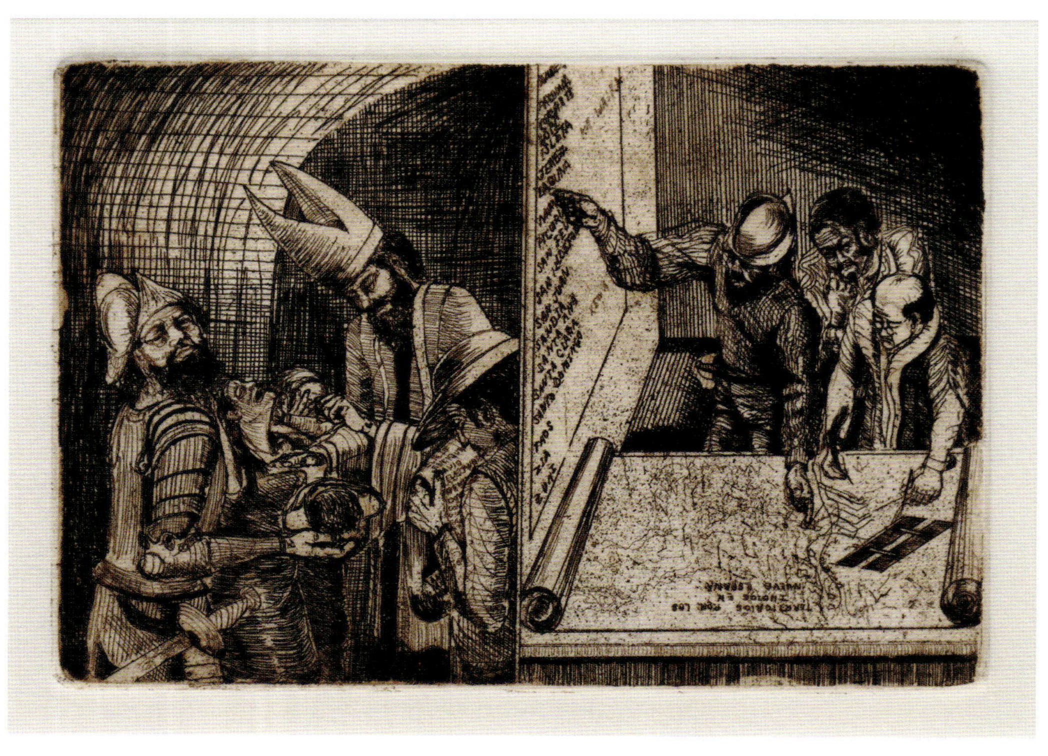

Figure 24. Floyd Solomon, *Erasing the Culture, Renaming the Children, Tribes and Lands,* undated. Etching, 4 ⅞ × 7 in. Collection of Jeanne Solomon Bell. Image courtesy of Geistlight Photography, Albuquerque, NM.

dispossession. It has given me a broader and deeper comprehension of the fragility of indigenous culture today. Most importantly, it helped me understand my inner self and to start the process of reconnecting to my heritage" (Solomon, Artist Statement).

Visualizing the dark episodes of the initial Spanish encounter, the subsequent revolt, and continuing governmental attempts to destroy Pueblo culture was not a nostalgic endeavor for Solomon. This was a contemporary project that brought the past into the present. He did not end the series with the Spanish but moved well into the twentieth century. This was part of the narrative, of course, but it was also a way to connect the past to the present and, most importantly for him, to bring the younger Pueblo generations into the flow of the narrative—he considered etching an effective means to stimulate and encourage younger Pueblo people to "pay attention and absorb our own history" (Solomon, Artist Statement). Fear that they would forget this important legacy fueled the project. Printmaking also allowed him to create multiples of his images and thus make them more widely available than single paintings would have been.

Solomon wrote about the cycle of prints as comprised of three distinct sections: "The first part illustrates the conquest on all levels of human exploitation and the Pueblos' subsequent adaptation to suppression. The second reveals the effects of US legislative actions imposed on Pueblos without proper representation. The third addresses the process of institutionalized assimilation and the gradual replacement of traditional government. It also touches on the ongoing exploitation of natural resources of Pueblo lands" (Solomon, Artist Statement). Sixteen of the intended larger series of prints for *Crucifixion of a Culture* were printed in 1995 and exhibited at the Wheelwright Museum of the American Indian in Santa Fe. These demonstrate that he had completed far more of the first part of the series, with its intense focus on Spanish brutality and the Pueblo uprising. A portion of the second section he envisioned is included here. The third remains unexplored in the thorough way he would have addressed it. However, from the power of the first and the portion of the second segments of the visual narrative, we can be certain that the third would have continued the force present in the previous images. Some images from the series were also exhibited in April 2000 at Highlands University in conjunction with a conference entitled

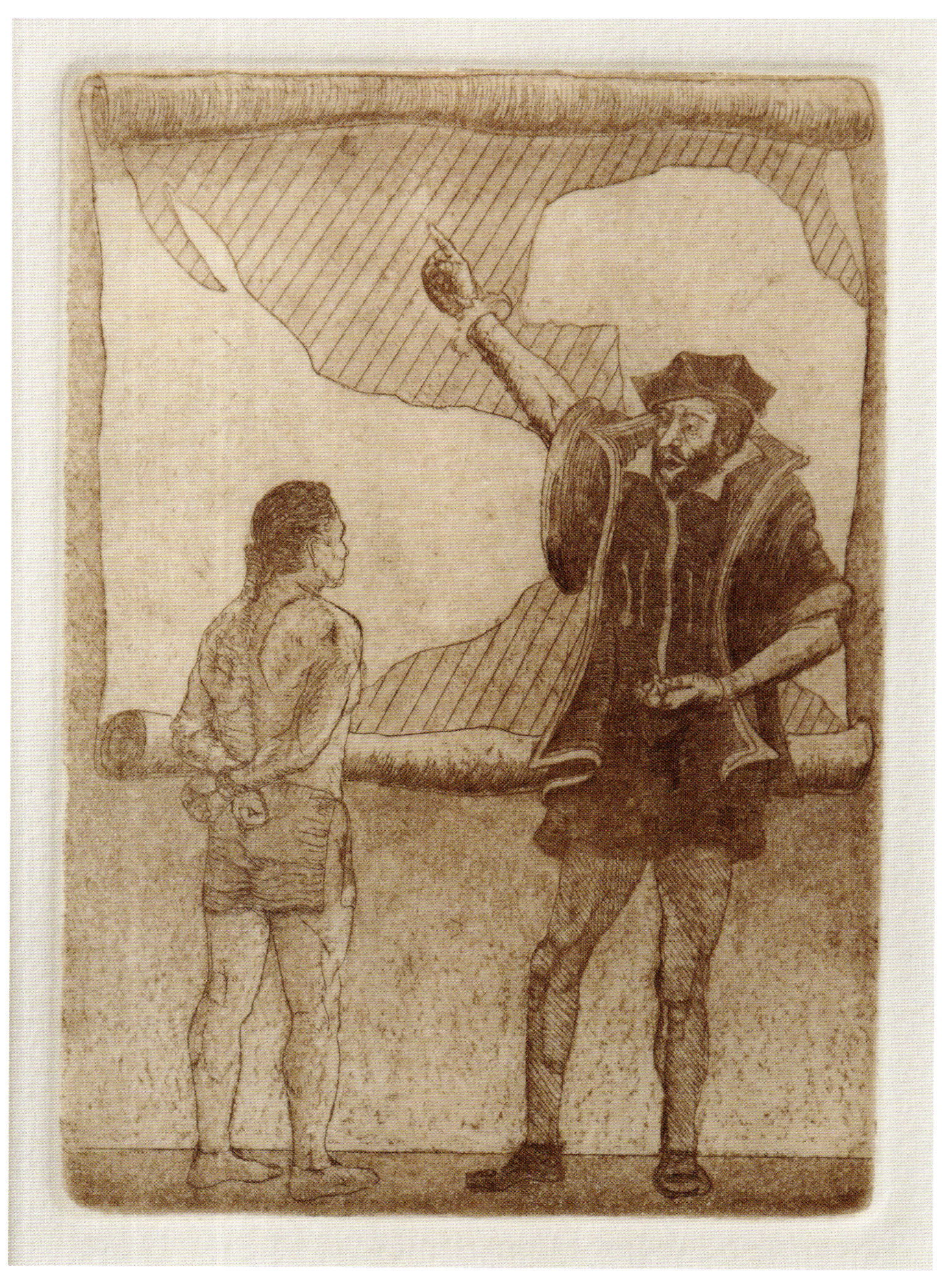

Figure 25. Floyd Solomon, *This Land Is Your Land, This Land Is My Land,* undated. Etching, 6 ⅞ × 3 ¾ in. Collection of Jeanne Solomon Bell. Image courtesy of Geistlight Photography, Albuquerque, NM.

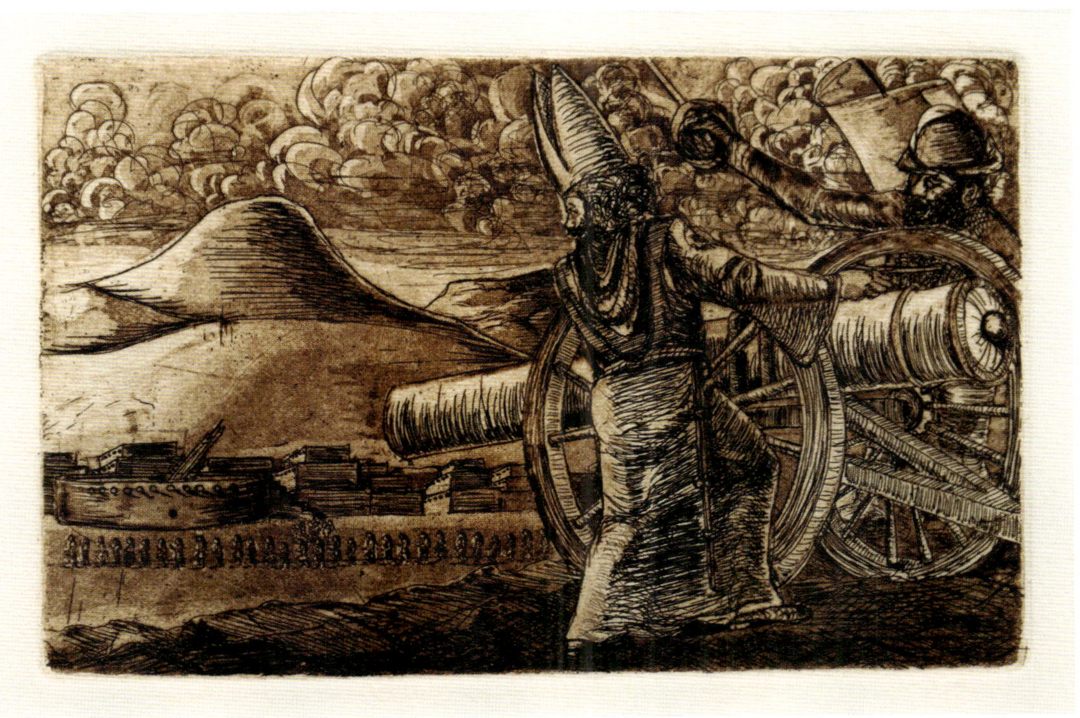

Figure 26. Floyd Solomon, *Selecting a Church Site,* undated. Etching, 4 ⅞ × 7 ½ in. Collection of Jeanne Solomon Bell. Image courtesy of Geistlight Photography, Albuquerque, NM.

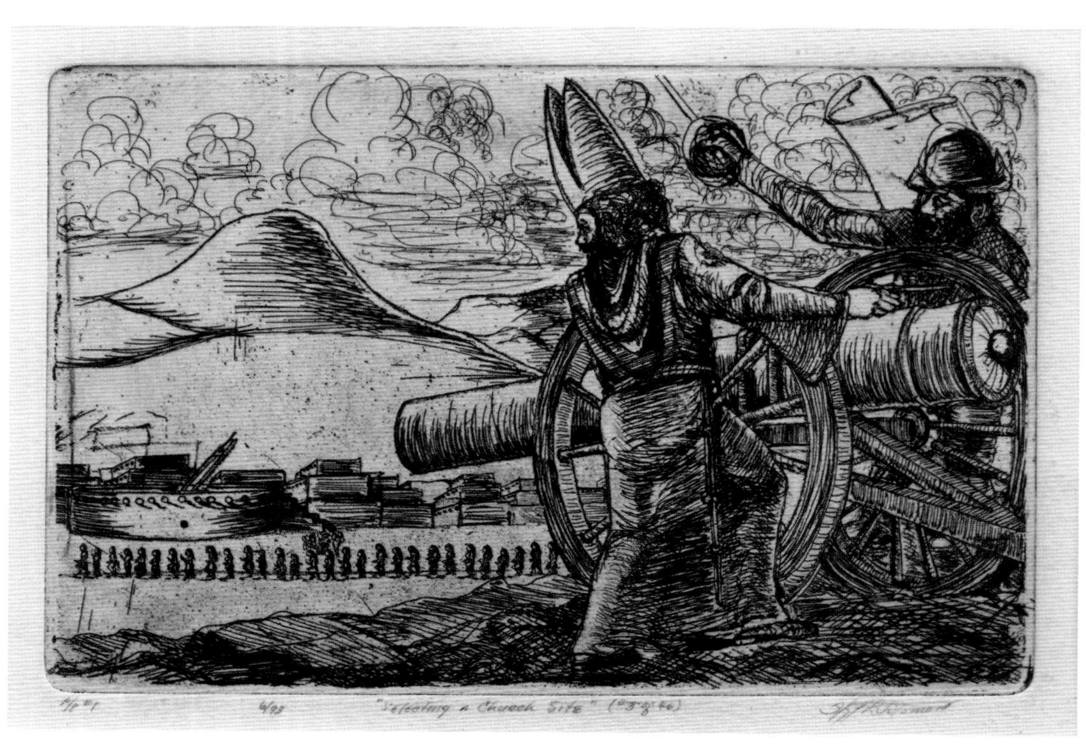

Figure 27. Floyd Solomon, *Selecting a Church Site,* undated. Etching, 4 ⅞ × 7 in. Collection of Jeanne Solomon Bell. Image courtesy of Geistlight Photography, Albuquerque, NM.

"Contemporary Vantage on the Coronado Expedition through Documents and Artifacts" (Flint 2017). Solomon spoke at the conference about his etchings and the view they provided of what he called the conquest. An exhibition of Solomon's work entitled *Art through Struggle* was also held at the Indian Pueblo Cultural Center in 2015.

Crucifixion of a Culture

Floyd Solomon left no known record of the order in which the prints comprising *Crucifixion of a Culture* were to be arranged. Some obviously predate the Pueblo Revolt of 1680, while others could be before, during, or after that historic event. Linearity was not vital to his narrative just as it is not in various Pueblo stories. The brutality the artist portrayed occurred both before and after the revolt, arguably more intensely following the return of the Spanish to the Southwest in 1692.

The Shaman's Dream foretells the rampage and destruction to come with the Spanish. Fantastic figures comingle with natural ones as Death appears in the front of the sinuous line of riders, its skeletal body here partially covered by a cloak. Behind, uniformed soldiers ride, one carrying a flag of the Spanish crown, and a figure carrying a cross and wearing a bishop's miter accompanies them. Winged figures, like harpies or demons, appear as well. A huge scaled, winged, and double-headed dragon-like form dominates the image, its curving body providing the unifying element for the much smaller figures included here. The shaman of Solomon's title appears below along the horizontal plane of the print, his back to the viewer. While his position suggests one of calm composure, what his dream reveals is anything but tranquil. His subconscious reveals horrors previously unknown and unimaginable to the Pueblo people. While powerful, he can do nothing to stop what will come with contact between the Spanish and the Pueblos beginning in 1539. Subsequent expeditions, both military and missionary, also brought settlers into the region by the late sixteenth century.

Contemplating Visual Symbols seems to repeat the theme in a calmer manner. Here the church, represented through a miter and a staff with a cross, and soldiers, who are represented by a helmet, appear in front of two Native men who look down toward the small fire burning in the bottom-left portion of the

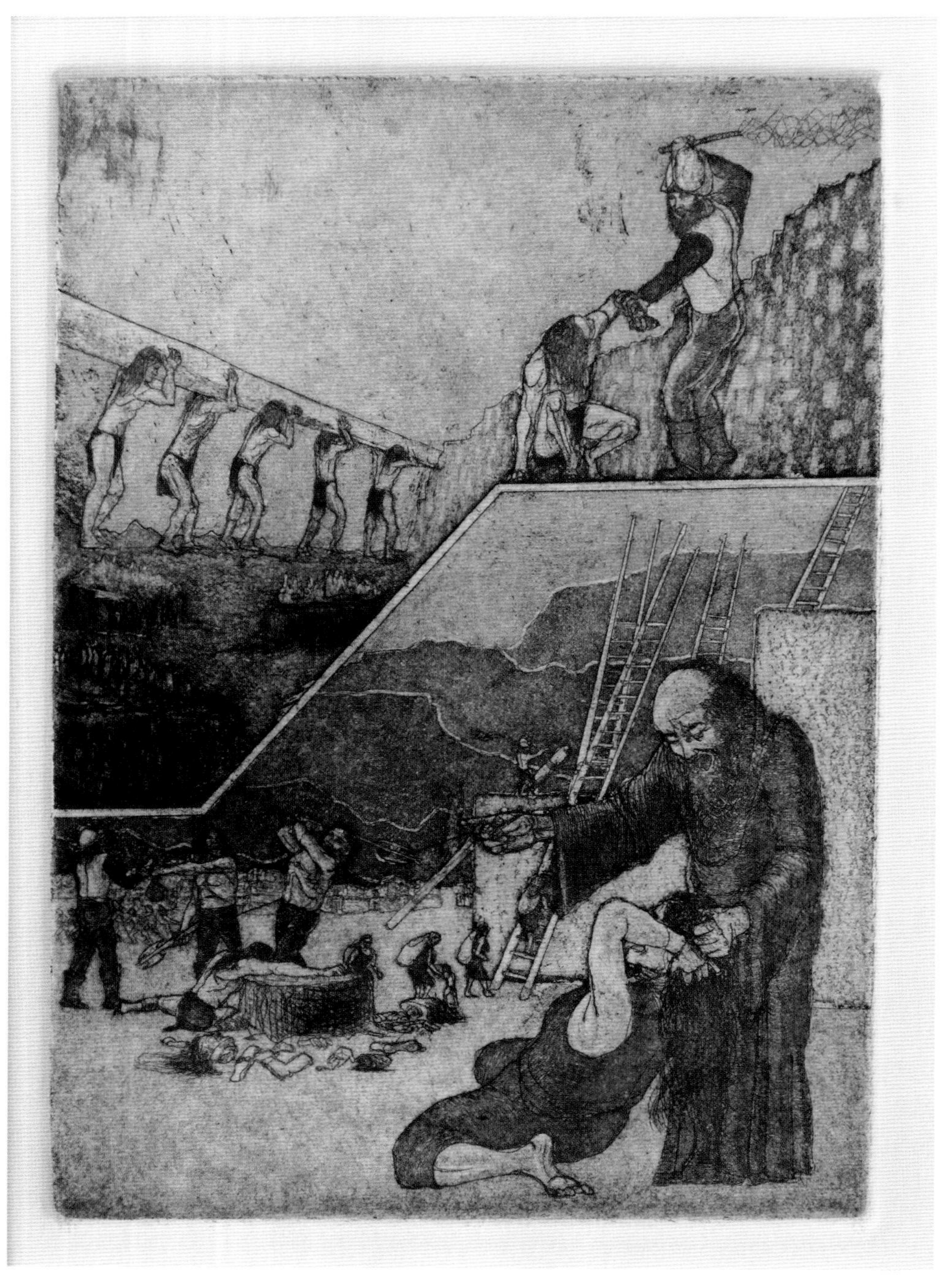

Figure 28. Floyd Solomon, *Building a Church*, undated. Etching, 6 ⅞ × 4 13⁄16 in. Collection of Jeanne Solomon Bell. Image courtesy of Geistlight Photography, Albuquerque, NM.

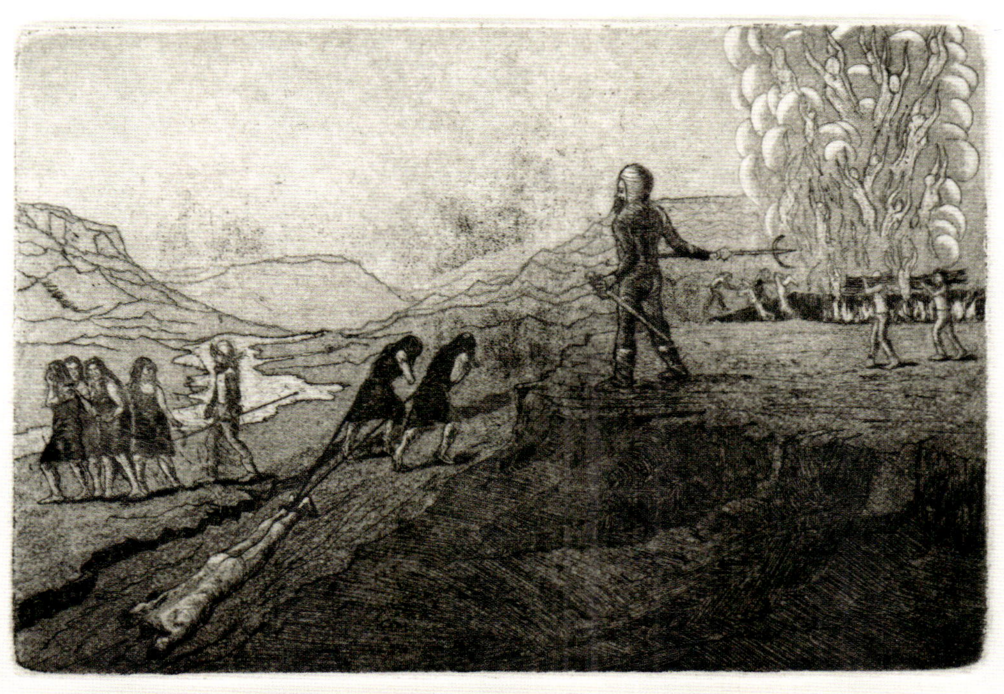

Figure 29. Floyd Solomon, *Destroying the Evidence*, undated. Etching, 4 ¾ × 6 ⅞ in. Collection of Jeanne Solomon Bell. Image courtesy of Geistlight Photography, Albuquerque, NM.

image. While the flames themselves are active, it is the billowing smoke that provides the most dramatic element here. To which part of the period this image refers to—from the arrival of the Spanish to their return and the events that followed—is unknown; its contemplative stance could relate to many times in the era of encounters between Pueblo and Spanish people.

Erasing the Culture, Renaming the Children, Tribes and Lands employs a two-part composition commemorating the importance of language and names that the Spanish sought to eradicate. The left-hand portion of the diptych presents a baby held in the hands of a Spanish soldier who clearly finds his proximity to the child disgusting as he turns his head away from the baby and its agonized relatives. A second Spaniard holds a scroll of possible names, from which the church official is bestowing one on the child he baptizes. Will this boy become known as David? Comments in Solomon's sketchbook explore the issue of naming in his own time as he asked, "Did you name your children after your oppressors? Why don't you use your Indian name? What is your *Indian* name?" Here again he brings the issues into the contemporary world.

The right half of the etching illustrates the renaming of the pueblos themselves. The soldier points to the list of new names for the communities while two officials examine a map of the Indian territories of New Spain, aligning the geographic locations with the new names assigned to them. Relabeling land is, of course, a way of extending control over it, of claiming that space for another culture. The same is true of the renaming of people—attempting to erase original names and replace them with new ones in the language of the dominant culture. Expunging language is at the very foundation of colonialization.

Building on the obvious idea of colonialization, *This Land Is Your Land, This Land Is My Land* illustrates a Spaniard pointing to a map of the western hemisphere as if to educate the Pueblo man in front of him about the vastness of the space around him and probably the power of the Spanish to control this territory. The relative scale of the figures and the open mouth of the Spaniard combine with the fine attire of the latter man versus the simple dress of the Native man to underscore the invader's relative importance as they perceived it.

Basically a self-taught printmaker, Solomon experimented with the medium. Two versions of several images from *Crucifixion of a Culture* exist.

Selecting a Church Site foregrounds a figure representing the Church directing that a canon fire on and destroy a kiva so that a church can be built on its site. Another print of the same subject uses a different colored ink. There are various other examples of Solomon's use of brown and black ink in his work, but, for this image, the artist ultimately determined that black ink, with its heightened impact and drama, was more effective in achieving his goals.

Missionization required churches, and the physical placement of those churches on the locations of Pueblo ritual chambers sent a clear sign that the new religion was supplanting the old. As the canon is readied for its task, minutely rendered people come from the pueblo to join the line of pueblo people already moving right to left across the pictorial space. Here, as indicated by Solomon's title, it is ground that must be cleared for the church to be built, and that construction will undoubtedly require more space than that taken up by the circular kiva visible in the sights of the canon. Other portions of the pueblo will be lost during this attack. Spanish forces and missionaries burned villages repeatedly after their arrival in the region, not only to clear space for the construction of the buildings they required as they imposed their faith on the Pueblo people but also in punishment for the actions of people who were accused of wrongdoing or who did not follow the laws imposed by the newcomers. The number of pueblos was dramatically diminished (Sando 1992, 78).

In order to construct the necessary new religious structures, friars forced Pueblo people to work gathering materials and raising missions. As with *Renaming the Children, Tribes and Lands,* Solomon divided the pictorial space of *Building a Church*. Here he used a hard, precise line to demarcate an upper segment filled with a depiction of the labor of Pueblo men who build the mission church. Five men moving from left to right carry a heavy beam while a Spanish soldier whips another man to the right. These two figures are positioned as if standing on higher ground or a platform. Below them and the men carrying materials for the church is the horrific scene of limbs being cut from Pueblo men who have not followed orders or have not converted. The priest in the foreground grasps a woman by her hair, pulling her back, and forces her to watch as some of the men of the village undergo this fate.

Brutal punishments inflicted on Pueblo people included amputations, the most well-known being that which occurred at Acoma in the late sixteenth

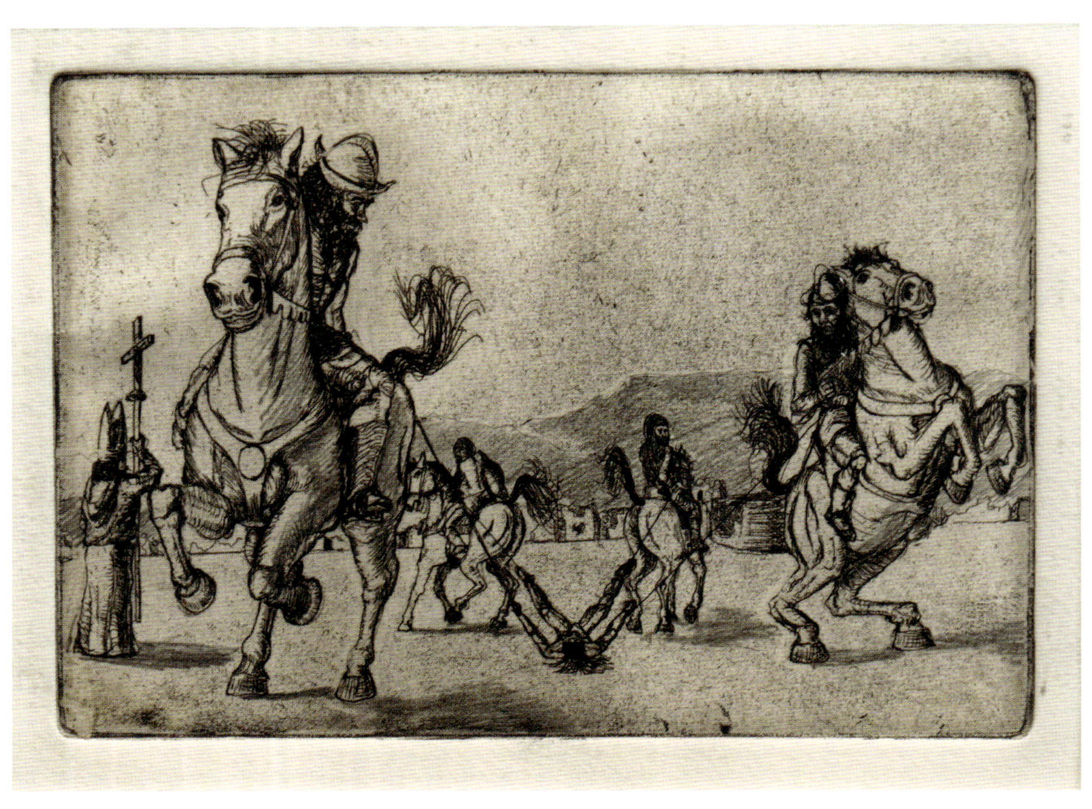

Figure 30. Floyd Solomon, *Convert or Die*, undated. Etching, 4 7/8 × 6 7/8 in. Collection of Jeanne Solomon Bell. Image courtesy of Geistlight Photography, Albuquerque, NM.

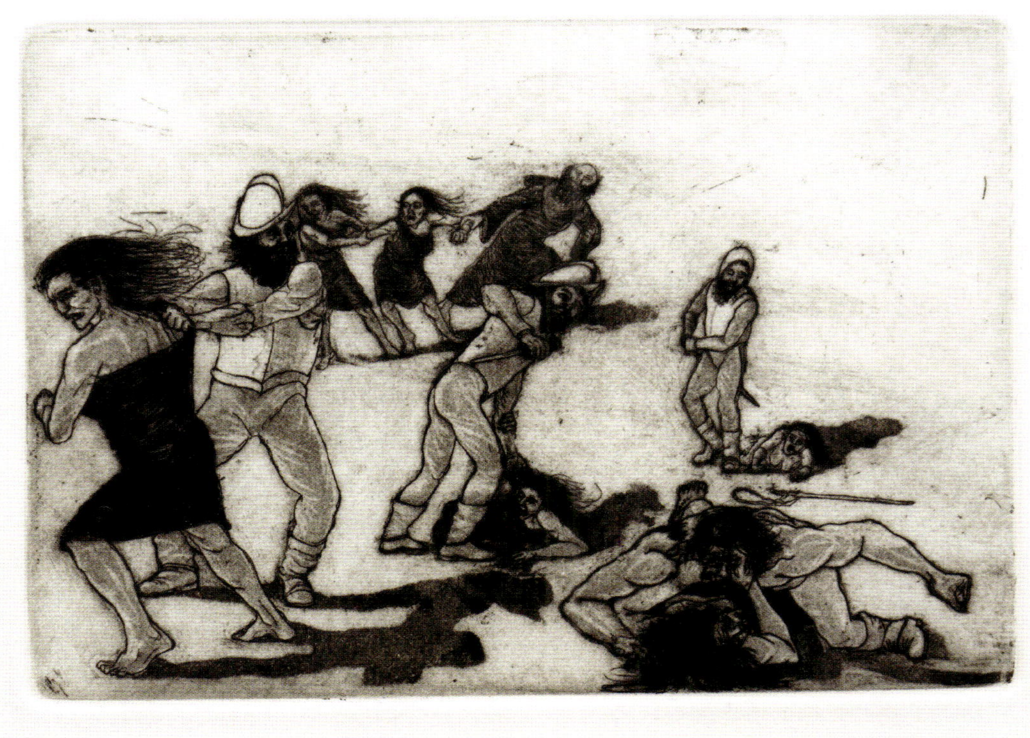

Figure 31. Floyd Solomon, *Bastardization*, 1994. Etching, 4 ⅞ × 6 13⁄16 in. Collection of Jeanne Solomon Bell. Image courtesy of Geistlight Photography, Albuquerque, NM.

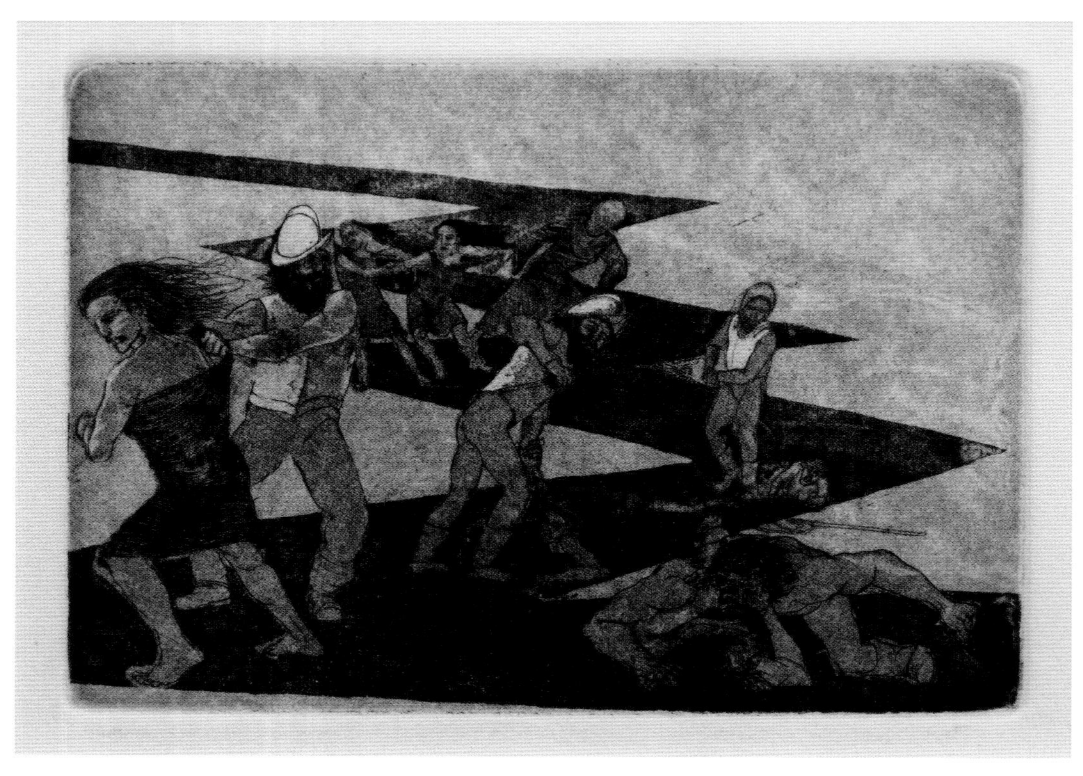

Figure 32. Floyd Solomon, *Untitled*, undated. Etching, 4 7⁄8 × 6 13⁄16 in. Collection of Jeanne Solomon Bell. Image courtesy of Geistlight Photography, Albuquerque, NM.

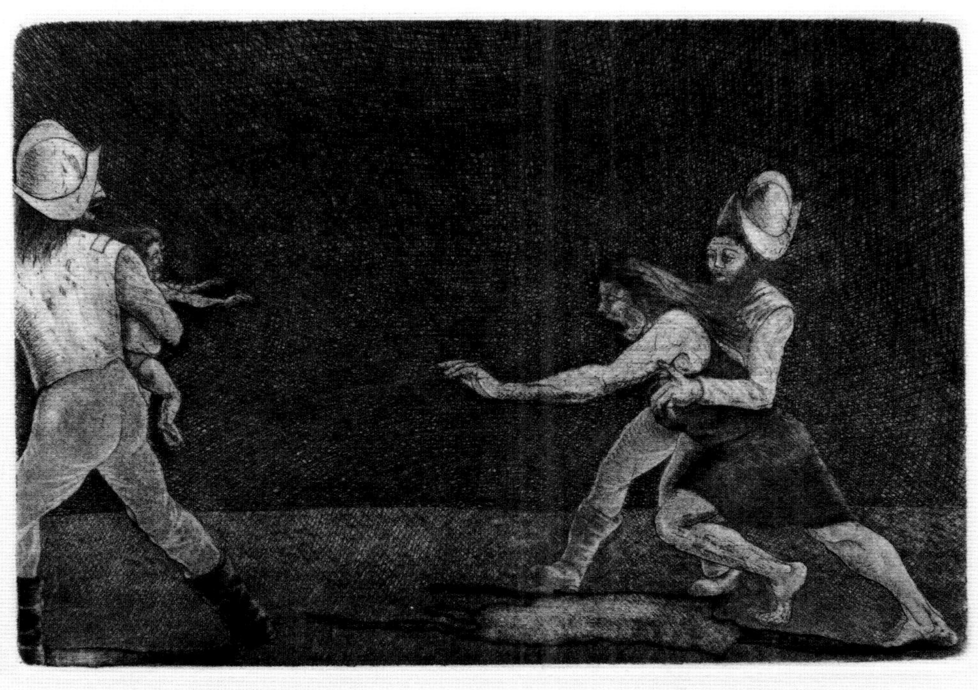

Figure 33. Floyd Solomon, *The Children Were Taken Away by the Spanish*, undated. Etching, 4 13⁄16 × 6 7⁄8 in. Collection of Jeanne Solomon Bell. Image courtesy of Geistlight Photography, Albuquerque, NM.

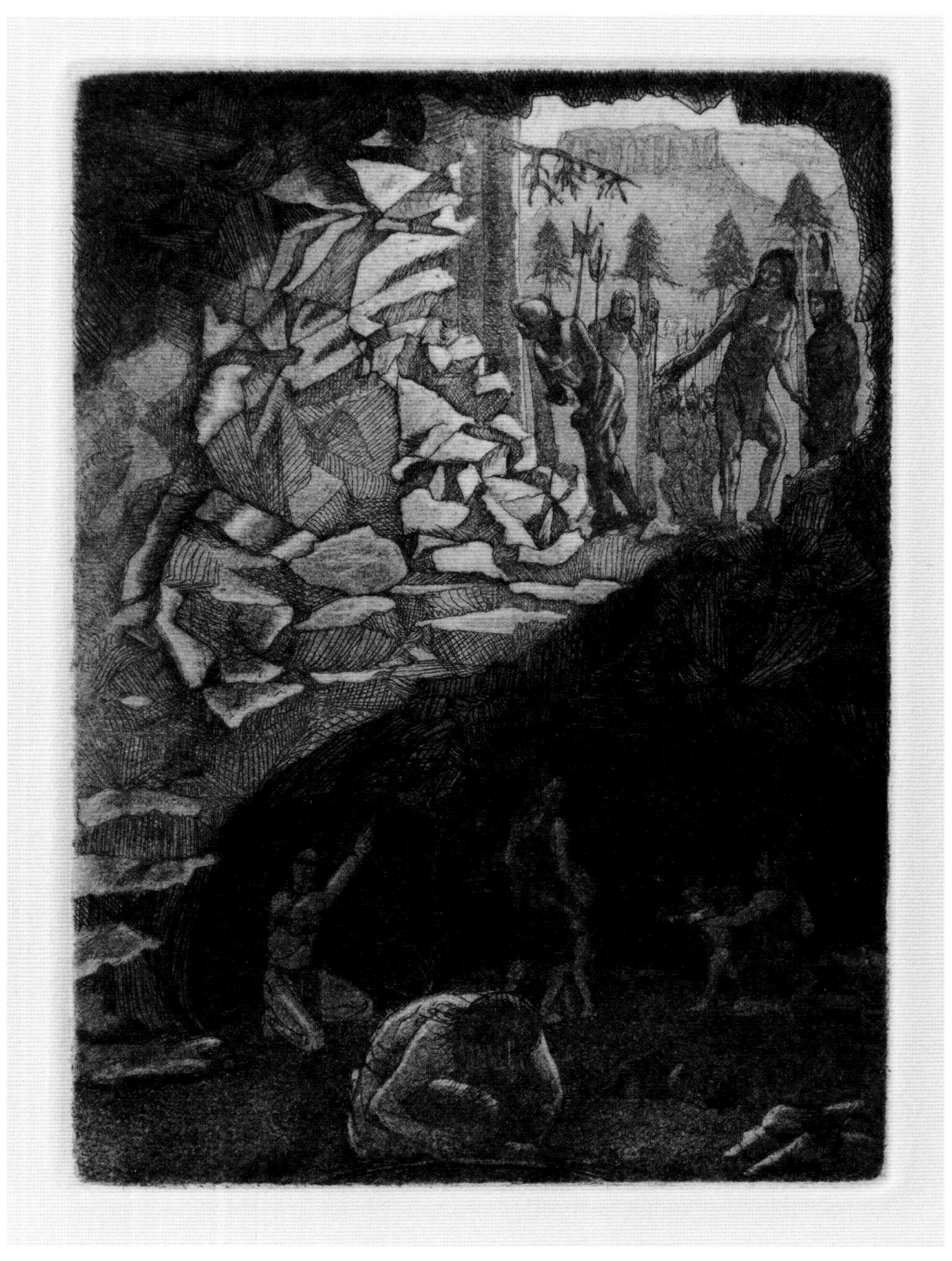

Figure 34. Floyd Solomon, *Traitor*, undated. Etching, 6 13⁄16 × 4 7⁄8 in. Collection of Jeanne Solomon Bell. Image courtesy of Geistlight Photography, Albuquerque, NM.

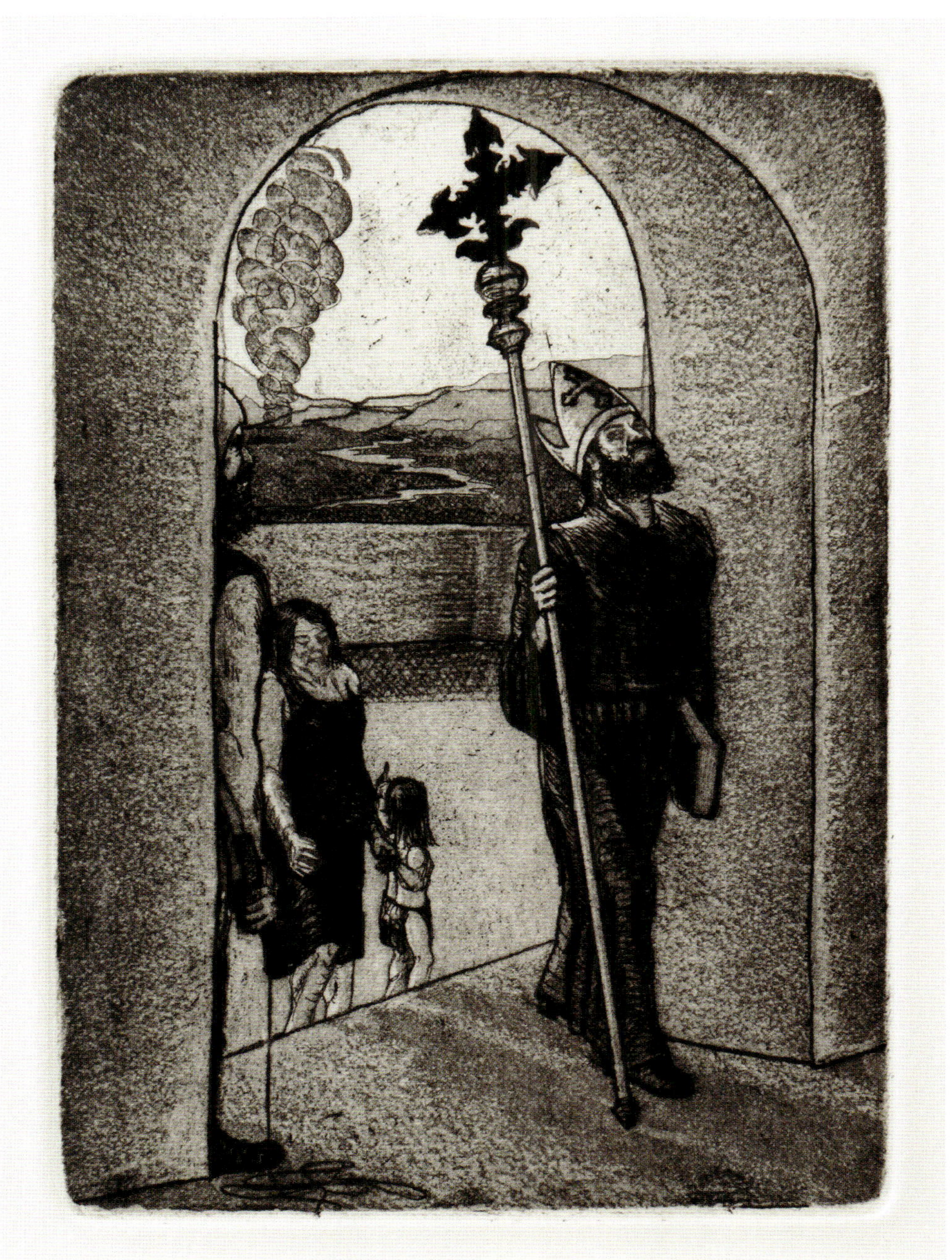

Figure 35. Floyd Solomon, *When the Saints Go Marching In*, undated. Etching, 6 13⁄16 × 4 7⁄8 in. Collection of Jeanne Solomon Bell. Image courtesy of Geistlight Photography, Albuquerque, NM.

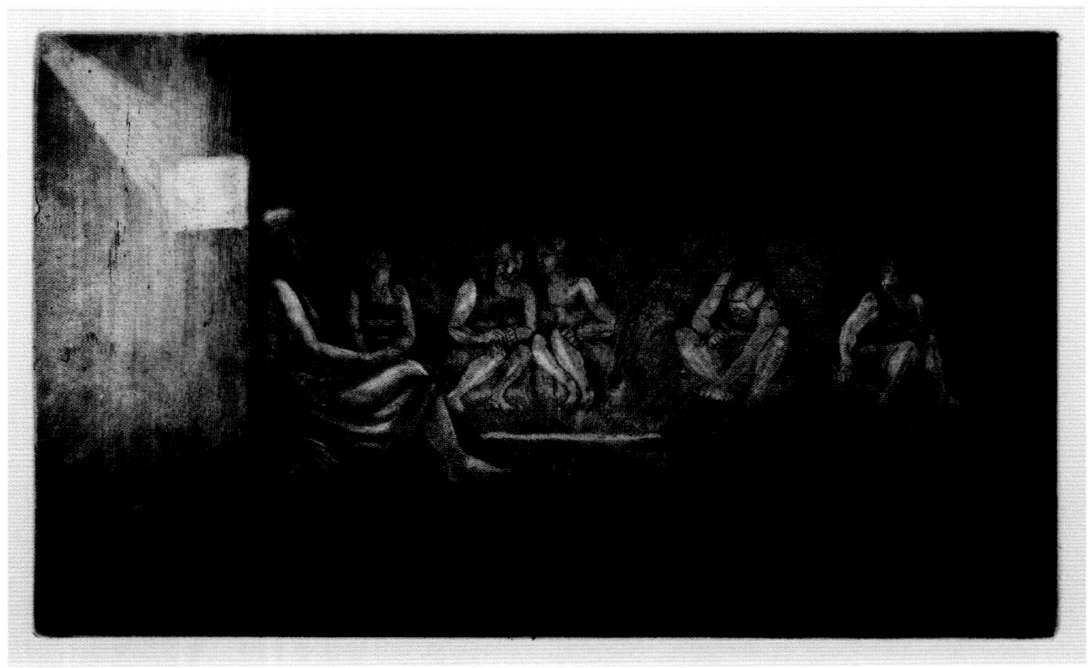

Figure 36. Floyd Solomon, *Kiva*, undated. Etching, 7 ¾ × 12 ¾ in. Collection of Jeanne Solomon Bell. Image courtesy of Geistlight Photography, Albuquerque, NM.

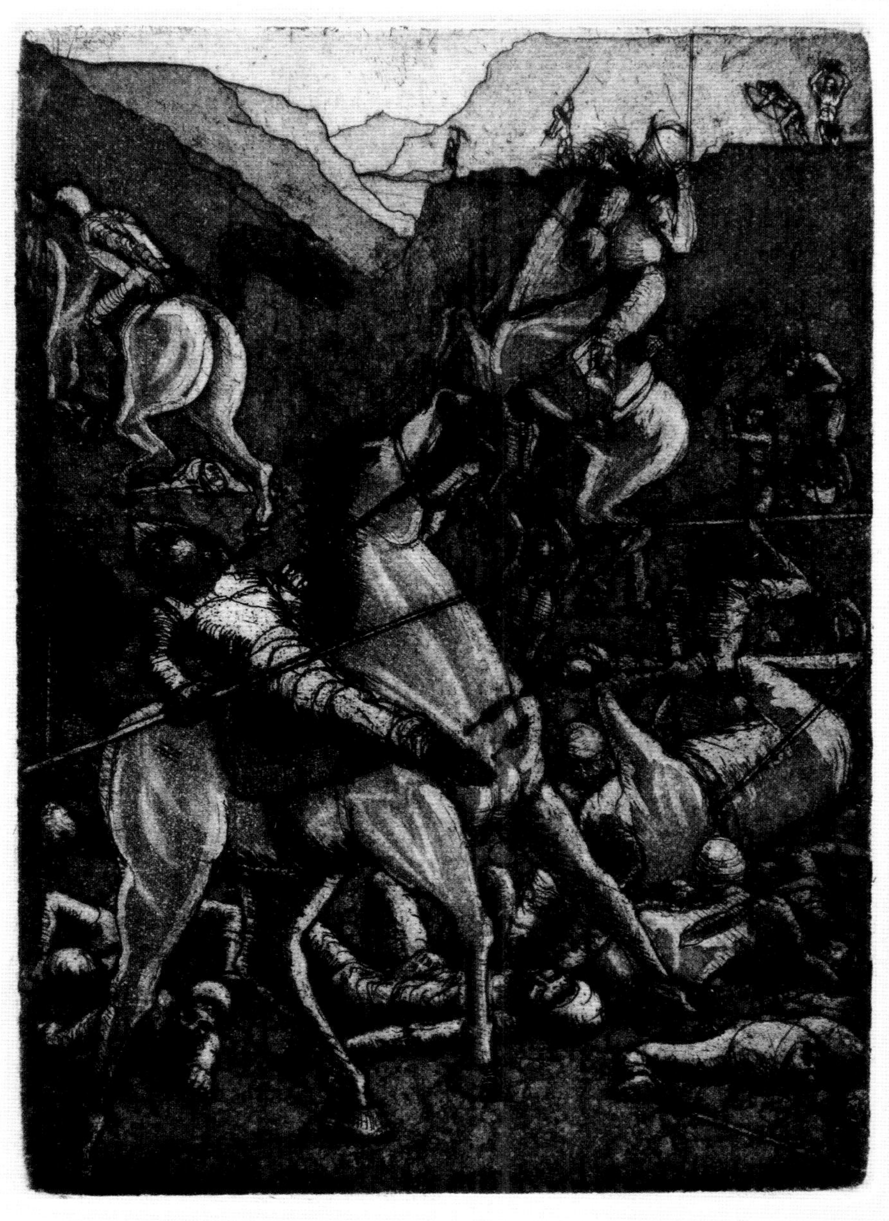

Figure 37. Floyd Solomon, *1680—The Pueblo Revolt,* undated. Etching, 6 13⁄16 × 4 13⁄16 in. Collection of Jeanne Solomon Bell. Image courtesy of Geistlight Photography, Albuquerque, NM.

century when Don Juan de Oñate ordered that the people of the pueblo be punished for resisting Spanish forces under the command of his nephew, who was killed during the resulting battle. One of the feet of every Acoma was amputated; some men had hands amputated as well. Additional offenses for which the Spanish exacted severe retribution included failure to pay the required tribute and follow religious and secular rules. Lashing, imprisonment, and hanging were also among Spanish responses to Pueblo refusals to conform. Ultimately Oñate was himself prosecuted for use of excessive force against the Pueblo people and other offenses, resulting in his expulsion from New Mexico.

Pueblo women in clear distress are forced to drag the mutilated body of a Pueblo man who has been executed by the Spanish to a raging bonfire in *Destroying the Evidence*. Four other women are forced to turn away from the destruction, without doubt to return to bring yet more bodies to burn. The fully landscaped setting includes rocky outcroppings and distant views that suggest the vastness of the area. Two men bring more fuel for the fire, and another Spanish soldier watches as the mutilated bodies of Pueblo men burn. Here the smoke from the inferno takes the form of human bodies, as if spirits of the murdered Pueblo people are emerging from the flames to rise above the conflagration. A telling preparatory sketch exaggerates the human forms in the flames even more pointedly, their slender bodies with upraised arms rising from the fire. The movement of the flames is reminiscent of some of work of the English poet, painter, and printmaker William Blake (1757–1827). His illustrations for *Songs of Innocence* are his most famous, and the comparison here is an important one that underscores the innocence of the Pueblo people in this specific instance and in many other encounters Solomon detailed.

In *Convert or Die*, one of his most powerful images, Solomon depicts the extremes to which the Spanish went in their missionization process. A Pueblo man is being pulled apart, his arms and legs tied to ropes, each held by an individual soldier who strains against the man. Unwilling converts were tortured, even to being drawn and quartered as Solomon suggests, and many died rather than surrender their own beliefs.

Other aspects of the dark days of which Solomon spoke are strongly indicated in *Bastardization*. Two versions of the same image included here highlight Solomon's experimentation with intaglio. In one, he has used aquatint to render the shadows of the figures, both the women who attempt to flee their attackers and the Spanish who rape them. The subject itself is a horrendous one made more powerful by the postures of the figures included. A second version of the print includes heavier use of aquatint in a bold zigzag pattern that recedes into space. That addition enhances the powerful impact of the print in various ways as it echoes the positions of the figures while its angularity underscores the brutality of the scene.

It was not only the adults who came under the harsh conditions imposed by the Spanish but also children. *The Children Are Taken Away* references the removal of children from their families and the enforced instruction of the next generation in the ways of the Spanish. The agony of this separation is made clear in the postures of both the mother and her child as one soldier carries the child away while another holds the mother back as she reaches toward her child, her muscles obviously straining in her full effort to prevent this additional horror. Solomon's use of dark aquatint and the dark outline of the misshapen shadow add to the dramatic content.

Traitor once again illustrates Solomon's experiments with space. Not only has the artist created a multiple-part space with the soldiers and traitor above and those hiding below, but the manner in which he has represented the rocks within this shelter recall some of the cubist experiments in his sketchbooks. The result is an emotionally powerful work that relays some of the blackest moments of the early years of Spanish interaction with Pueblo people. "Traitor" refers to the Pueblo man seen standing at the entrance to the cave where other members of his community are secreted below. He has brought the Spanish soldiers here, betraying the men, women, and children, who appear faintly in the rich darkness of the cave. Solomon's use of multiple lines and heavy ink creates a stark contrast with the daylight-filled area at the entrance to the cavern. He heard stories of such Native traitors, and rather than eliminating them from his visual record, he included them in his attempt to relay as complete a narrative as possible. Such actions occurred at various times throughout the initial years of contact, during the Pueblo Revolt and immediately thereafter, and following the return of the Spanish to the Southwest. Some factions sided with the Spanish, even inviting them to return after the revolt, and certainly others betrayed members of their own villages as well as those from other pueblos (Sando 1992, 67–69).

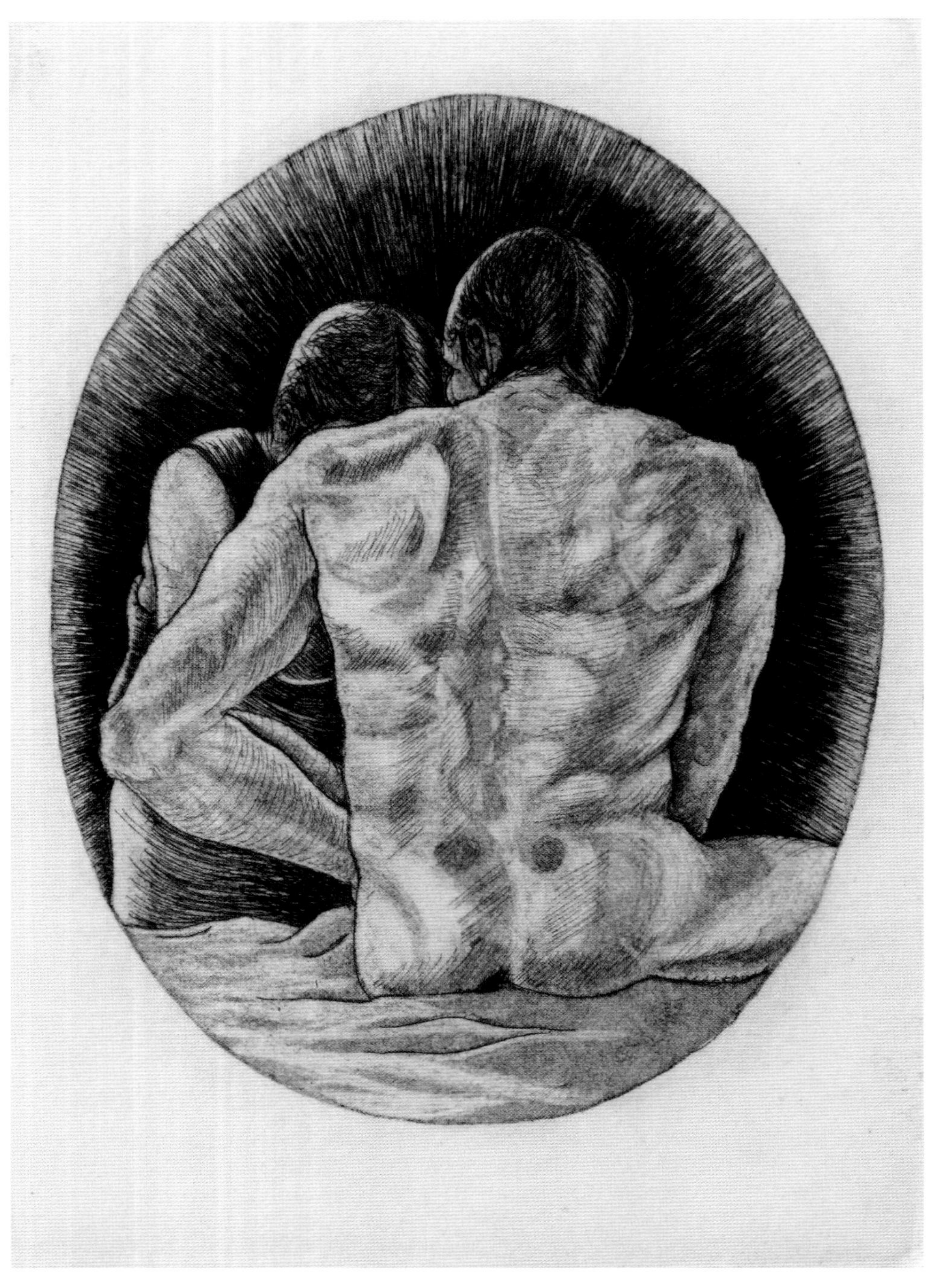

Figure 38. Floyd Solomon, *1680–1692—A Time to Heal*, undated. Etching, 6 ⅞ × 4 ⅞ in. Collection of Jeanne Solomon Bell. Image courtesy of Geistlight Photography, Albuquerque, NM.

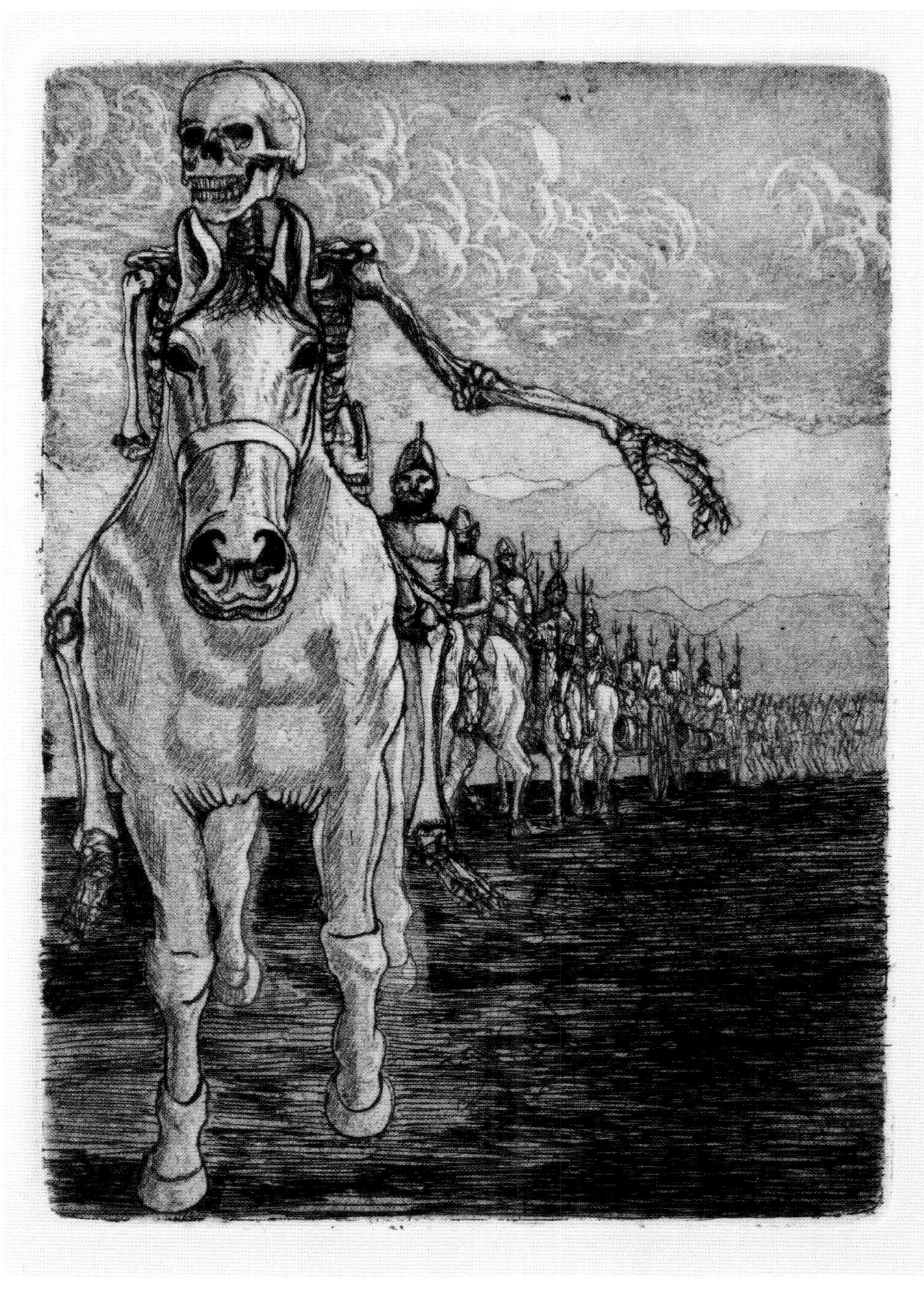

Figure 39. Floyd Solomon, *1692—The Return of Death,* undated. Etching, 6 ¾ × 4 ⅞ in. Collection of Jeanne Solomon Bell. Image courtesy of Geistlight Photography, Albuquerque, NM.

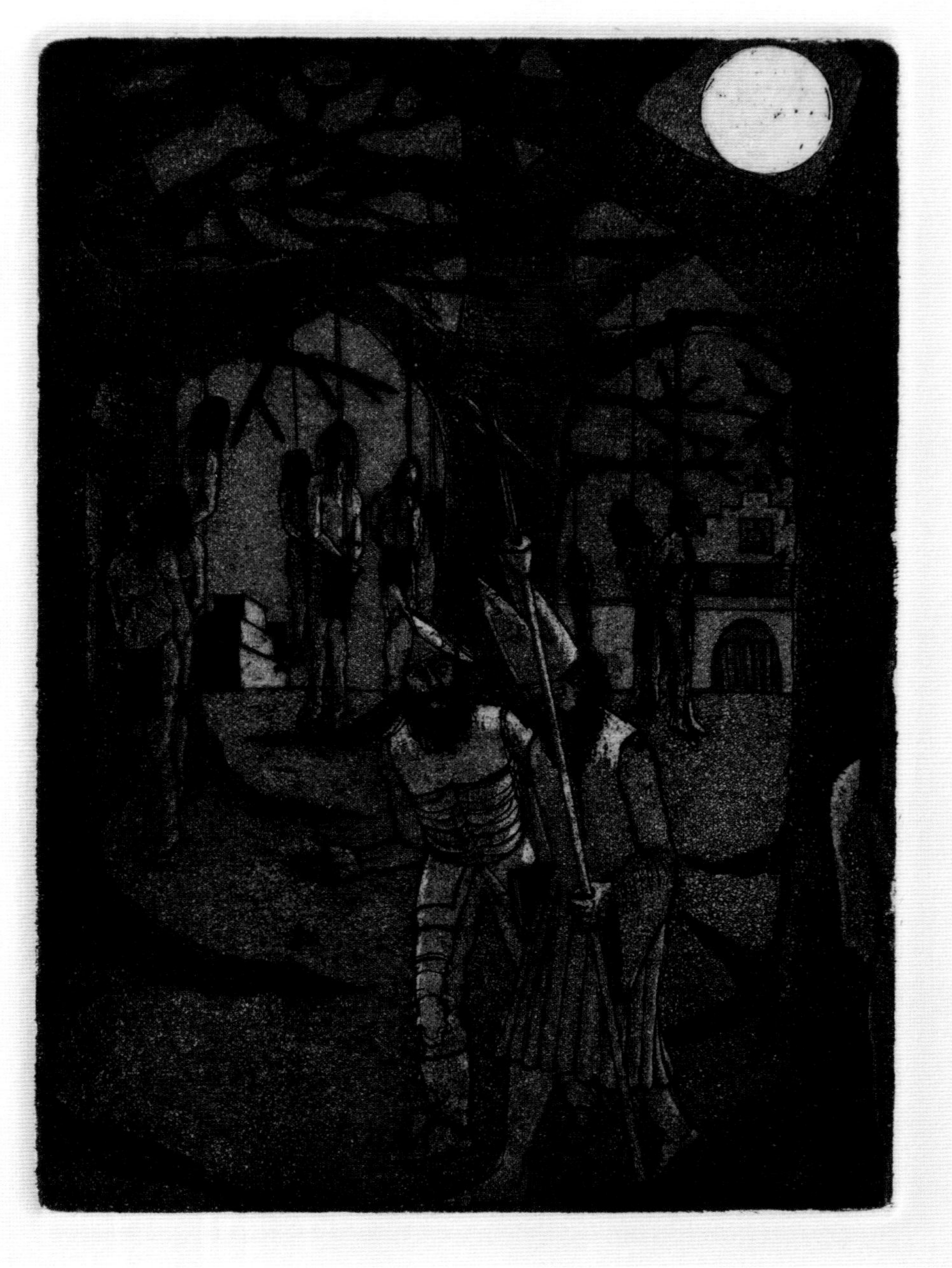

Figure 40. Floyd Solomon, *A Walk through the Hanging Gardens*, undated. Etching, 6 13⁄16 × 4 7⁄8 in. Collection of Jeanne Solomon Bell. Image courtesy of Geistlight Photography, Albuquerque, NM.

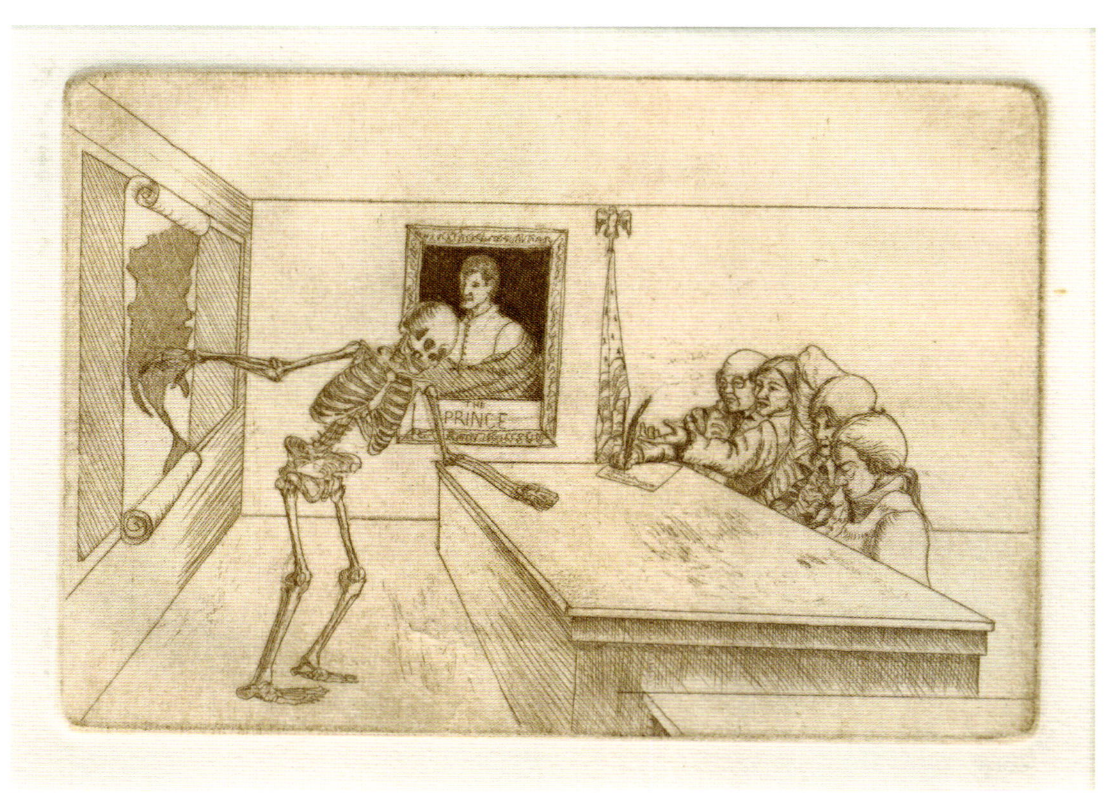

Figure 41. Floyd Solomon, *The Prince*, undated. Etching, 4 ¾ × 6 ⅞ in. Collection of Jeanne Solomon Bell. Image courtesy of Geistlight Photography, Albuquerque, NM.

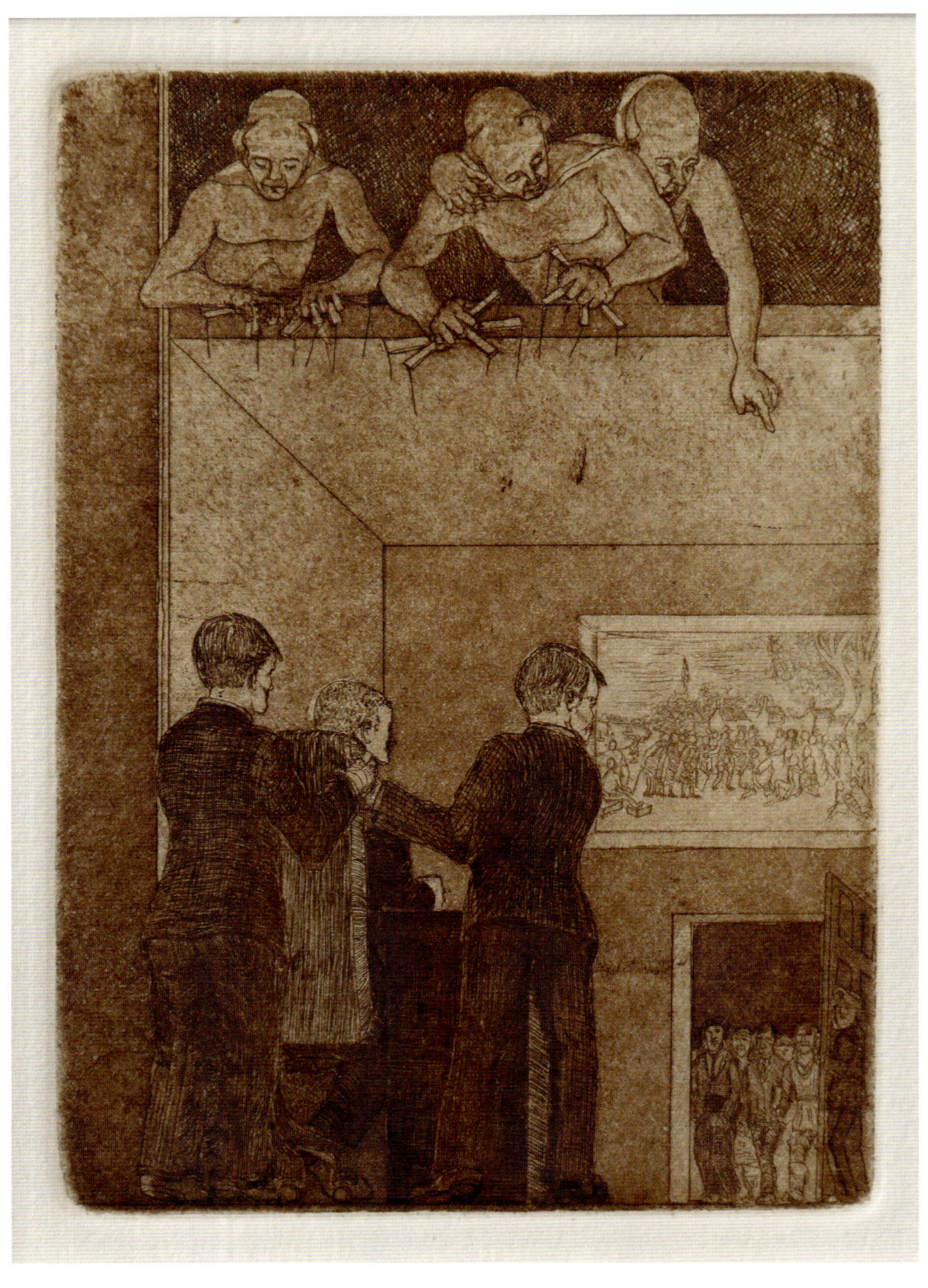

Figure 42. Floyd Solomon, *The Puppeteers*, undated. Etching, 6 ⅞ × 4 13⁄16 in. Collection of Jeanne Solomon Bell. Image courtesy of Geistlight Photography, Albuquerque, NM.

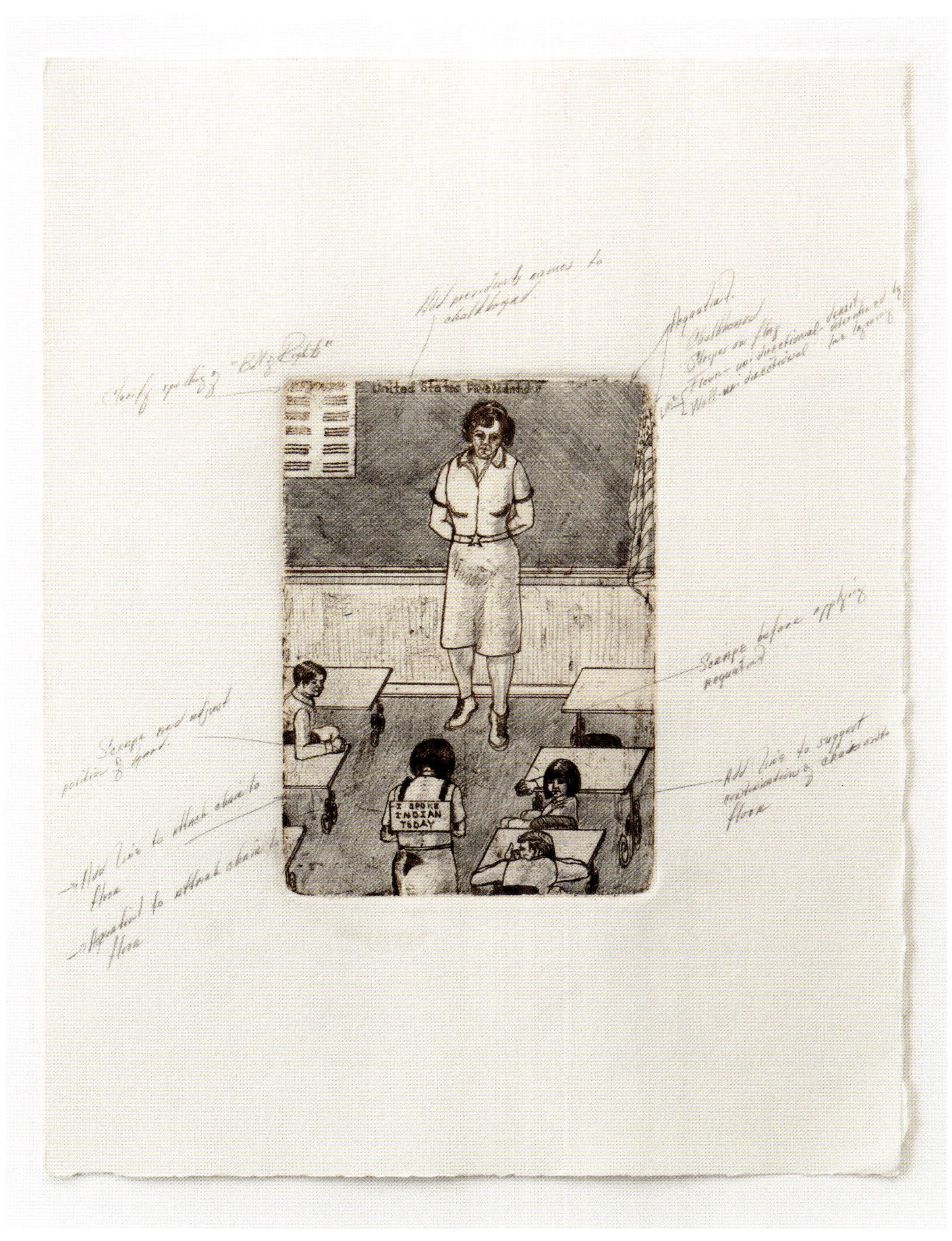

Figure 43. Floyd Solomon, *I Spoke Indian Today*, undated. Etching with graphite edits, 6 ⅞ × 4 ¾ in. Collection of Jeanne Solomon Bell. Image courtesy of Geistlight Photography, Albuquerque, NM.

When the Saints Go Marching In foregrounds a friar who holds a crucifix and carries a religious volume as he walks into a church followed by a Pueblo woman and child. A soldier stands to the far visual left, a whip apparent in his hand with its sinuous cords curling at the entrance to the church. The woman firmly clutches her child's hand as he turns to view a river in the distance as well as the heavy smoke from a fire. This fire undoubtedly alludes to the destruction of traditional Pueblo life and its replacement by a new one that will be dictated by the Church. Solomon's title surely does not reference the missionaries and soldiers but, rather, the Pueblo people who have been martyred for their beliefs and those people who also survive to maintain their culture.

Pueblo people, particularly women and children, attempted to hide from Spanish forces. *Kiva* records this reality, the darkness of the ink repeating the deep shadows within the structure in which they have taken refuge. The light that shines into the space from the upper left allows portions of six figures to be revealed, while the back wall and the floor remain in the velvety black of the ink Solomon used heavily.

The battle that rages in *The Pueblo Revolt* recalls Italian Renaissance master Paolo Ucello's (1397–1475) battle images, especially in Solomon's use of spears and fallen human bodies and horses in a complex rendition of linear perspective. Pueblo men fight from village walls, firing down on the enemy below with bows and arrows and lances. Another hurls a stone. Below, others brandish weapons as they fight Spanish soldiers who have fallen as well as others who remain mounted. Some Spaniards use the bodies of their contorted dead or dying horses as cover against the Pueblo men who have now organized to fight against them.

Solomon's strongly rendered horses, whose muscles strain in action and whose nostrils flare, effectively relay the fear experienced in intense battle. His complex composition combines multiple sharp diagonals of lances, horses, and humans, and it conveys a sense of the far larger numbers of figures involved and the actions and reactions of all depicted.

An extremely different tone is set by Solomon's work *1680–1692—A Time to Heal*. The man and woman positioned here are at least temporarily free from the conflicts that occurred between the arrival of the Spanish and before the Pueblo Revolt. They are also unaware of what is yet to come when the invaders once again return. While we do not see the obviously male figure from the front, the second figure appears to be tending to him. Perhaps he has been wounded and, thus, the title refers not only to emotional but also physical healing. The Pueblo people needed both, and the years between the Revolt and the return of the invaders allowed them to separate those practices enforced upon them by the Spanish and focus more fully on traditional lifeways. Solomon employed only two figures here in a rare exception to most of the rest of *Crucifixion of a Culture*, where more figures engage in the action depicted. He highlighted this image as well by presenting it in an oval composition rather than using the rectangular format of the remainder of the series. The dark background against which the figures are positioned provides a strong depth to the composition as the upper two-thirds of the oval lighten through parallel lines that draw the viewer further into the darkness.

Two of the most powerful images in Solomon's record are those of *1692—The Return of Death* and *A Walk through the Hanging Gardens*. Death in skeletal form leads a long line of Spanish soldiers in *The Return of Death*. Here, even the clearly articulated Death seems almost to be shedding a tear as the unending trail of Spaniards continues in its path to destroy Native people. Hatching on portions of the body of the horse that Death rides show a distinct representation of a cross, a reference to the intertwined nature of religion and force in seeking conquest of Native people of the Americas.

The composition here, with its grizzly death image, recalls many images from European art history, especially those of German printmaker Albrecht Dürer (1471–1528). Dürer's *Four Horsemen of the Apocalypse*, with figures receding diagonally into space, relays more force than Solomon's work, but the steady movement of the Spanish soldiers led by Death conveys the apparently unstoppable determination of these invaders who have both God, as evidenced by the cross, and death on their side.

A Walk through the Hanging Gardens, through the darkness of its subject with the mutilated bodies of Pueblo people suspended by ropes from trees and the heavy black ink used in the aquatint that played such a prominent role in the creation of the print itself, is perhaps the most somber work in the series. Those who walk, seemingly without care, through this garden of death are both church and military figures, again suggesting their joint guilt in the horrific scene recorded. Goya, too, created a print in his early nineteenth-century *Disasters of War* series that illustrates a French soldier casually leaning against a rock as he stares at the suspended body of a Spanish citizen who has been hung. While Goya's image is a strong suggestion of the inhumanity of war, Solomon's is much more intense.

In the artist's sketch for *A Walk through the Hanging Gardens*, four Pueblo men hang from tree limbs, back to back in two sets of pairs. Another figure is suspended in the margin outside the blocked pictorial space. Three or potentially four fully realized figures also hang to the right. A single armor-clad soldier and a churchman with a miter and cross walk away, their backs to the dead men. In the completed etching, Solomon added far more detail and more figures, eight or nine in total. The large tree, its branches heavy with the figures who hang from them, has roots that reach out to form a pathway and an arbor through which the soldier and missionary are passing, their postures implying a private conversation as if they are totally oblivious to the executions in which they have been involved. The background reveals that this carnage has taken place in front of the mission church itself, the structure apparent with its arched doorway, stepped roofline, and the bell that sits within a small opening on the upper level. A portion of the Pueblo stands in the left part of the background.

While Pueblo men were undoubtedly hung at various times for differing offenses, one noted occasion occurred in 1675 when, as Joe Sando records, forty-seven Pueblos were accused of sorcery and murder. Three were publicly hung in their respective pueblos of Jemez, Nambe, and San Felipe. Sando lists the memory of these deaths as "the first flames of revolt," and, as he wrote in the early 1990s, "it lives in the hearts of the people even now" (Sando 1992, 63). Solomon has not recorded that specific event as Sando relates it, but he has presented a startling view of the horrors that the Pueblo people suffered.

Four men dressed in American colonial or revolutionary attire sit behind a desk in *The Prince*. An American flag appears to the left of the desk, and a portrait labeled "The Prince" is on the wall beyond the flag. The men appear to be listening to a skeletal figure of death who points to a map of North America. While the full context here is unknown, Solomon's intention of carrying the themes of *Crucifixion of a Culture* into the elimination of the rights of Native people well beyond the Spanish encounters in the Southwest is clear.

Two prints, *Puppeteers* and especially *I Spoke Indian Today*, suggest a direction further prints would have taken. Three puppeteers, familiar from *Deceptus Magnus*, control actions below them in *Puppeteers*, while a group of young children in a school setting from the mid-twentieth century face their Anglo teacher in *I Spoke Indian Today*. The latter print also makes clear Solomon's intent to bring his series forward into more contemporary times. One of the students is being punished for having spoken her own language; she wears a sign on her back indicating her infraction of the rules imposed on Native students. The classroom itself is filled with signs of assimilation and the negation of Native history. The only history that matters here is suggested by the list of American presidents on the wall. That single-focused view of history is what Solomon fought against, using his strong artistic voice to increase our knowledge of the past. Those prints that he planned but ultimately left incomplete would certainly have expanded that reimagining of history in many more ways.

Conclusion

Floyd Solomon's exploration of the events surrounding the arrival of the Spanish in the Southwest, the Pueblo Revolt that drove the Spanish from the region, and the return of the invaders presents a powerful, very personal record of his views of those events. Many Native people today still recall that history. As the brief examination of some other modern and contemporary Native artists provided in chapter 2 suggests, those encounters fuel the subject matter that has been and continues to be explored. While relationships between cultures have improved dramatically over the centuries since the Spanish arrived, the memories and stories relayed in Native communities are strong.

Recent politicized events have taken issue with the glorification of conquistadores and their actions. The bronze figure of Juan de Oñate in Alcalde near where the conquistador founded the first Spanish settlement in New Mexico in 1598 was vandalized four hundred years later. In December 1997, one of Oñate's feet was cut from the equestrian statue. This was a symbolic reference to the fact that Oñate had ordered that one of the feet of each Acoma man of fighting age be amputated after their failed uprising against the Spanish in 1598. While no one is talking publicly about where that boot-clad foot is now, a September 2017 *New York Times* article shows a disguised man holding the right foot, complete with spur and stirrup. The unidentified man spoke with the reporter to emphasize the necessity of shaming, not honoring, Oñate. More recently the left foot, which remains on the monument, was painted red, and the words "Remember 1680," a reference to the Pueblo Revolt, were written on the monument's walls. A plaster replica of the right amputated foot was also on display at the art venue SITE in Santa Fe from August 2018 to January 2019 as part of its *Casa Tomada* (House Taken Over) exhibit. The meanings of these actions were and continue to be extremely clear.

Another repeated point of contention in Santa Fe has been the annual Santa Fe Fiesta that, until 2018, had included a reenactment of the reoccupation of Santa Fe by the Spanish under Diego José de Vargas in 1692. Negative responses to the event grew louder as Native people, Pueblos in particular, expressed their opinion that the Fiesta was presenting a false view of history. The event's organizers held that the Fiesta was a celebration of an agreement between the Spanish and the Pueblo people to live together peacefully, but many Pueblo people saw the event solely as a celebration of conquest and the repression of their cultures. In December of 2017, the All Pueblo Council of Governors unanimously endorsed a proclamation stating that the pageant did not portray the truth. This act of resistance was intended to disrupt the effects of acculturation by asserting cultural identity and survival. The Pueblo Council's act of defiance was supported by the archbishop of Santa Fe, John Wester, and the mayor of the city.

Three years of very active protests brought an end to the Entrada reenactment in 2018. An additional ceremony, Celebration of Community Faith, which honors various cultural traditions and "acknowledges the history of Santa Fe, recognizes shared values, and commits the community to the hard work of forgiveness and reconciliation" (Last 2018a) was incorporated into the Fiesta in September 2019. In concert with these changes, Santa Fe schools began limiting visits by reenactors of the Entrada to history classes—not, as previously, to the entire school (Last, 2018b). Thus, the current Fiestas de Santa Fe and their companion activities reflect continuing negotiations between cultures in the region. Not everyone is pleased with these compromises, but they reflect good-faith efforts to ease tensions.

Whenever cultures come in contact with each other in sometimes violent ways, memories remain strong. But the willingness to work toward common ground without losing vital connections to one's own heritage suggests the distance former enemies have come over the centuries. People of both Native and Spanish heritage share feast days, while Pueblos are claiming their right to rename themselves in their own languages.

Floyd Solomon would undoubtedly have been pleased with these changes, but he would have continued to advocate for more adjustments, for greater recognition of the history of Pueblo and Spanish encounters. Glorifications of conquistadores and reenactments of the Entrada would have been part of a vision of the past that removed the importance of Pueblo people from it. Solomon would have continued to use the strong voice of his art to relay what he felt were more accurate views of the distant past, but, as is evident in the last unfinished etching of his included here, *I Spoke Indian Today*, which showcases children in a classroom and a non-Native teacher as their instructor, he was looking well beyond the older stories of the Spanish arrival and their encounters with the Pueblos. He recognized that while much had changed, much remains to be addressed. He would have added his art and its accompanying voice to the demands for the cessation of Entrada reenactments as well as to other ways of proclaiming the continued strength and survival of Native people.

BIBLIOGRAPHY

Batkin, Jonathan. 1999. *Clay People, Pueblo Indian Figurative Traditions*. Santa Fe, NM: Wheelwright Museum of the American Indian.

Bell, Jeanne Solomon. 2012. Interview by Joyce M. Szabo, June 24.

Bennett, Meghan. 2018. "Santa Fe Ends Historic Fiesta Entrada—Organizers Drop Re-enactment of the 1692 Spanish Reoccupation of Santa Fe on the Plaza." *Albuquerque Journal*, July 26.

Carter, William B. 2009. *Indian Alliances and the Spanish in the Southwest, 750–1750*. Norman: University of Oklahoma Press.

Flint, Richard. 2002. *Great Cruelties Have Been Reported: The 1544 Investigation of the Coronado Expedition*. Dallas: Southern Methodist University Press.

———. 2008. *No Settlement, No Conquest: A History of the Coronado Entrada*. Albuquerque: University of New Mexico Press.

———. 2009. "Without Them, Nothing Was Possible: The Coronado Expedition's Indian Allies." *New Mexico Historical Review* 84, no. 1: 65–118.

———. 2017. Email correspondence to Joyce M. Szabo, July 19.

Giago, Denise. 2013. "Born with Clay in His Hands: Virgil Ortiz." In *Eyapaha Today*, September 2013. https://www.indianz.com/News/2013/011273.asp. Accessed 8/12/17.

Goldwater, Robert, and Marco Treves. 1975. *Artists on Art from the XIV to the XX Century*. New York: Pantheon Books.

Hackett, Charles Wilson. 1942. *Revolt of the Pueblo Indians of New Mexico and Otermin's Attempted Reconquest, 1680–1682*. Trans. Charmion Clair Shelby. 2 vols. Albuquerque: University of New Mexico Press.

Hammond, George P., and Agapito Rey. 1953. *Don Juan de Oñate: Colonizer of New Mexico, 1595–1628*. 2 vols. Albuquerque: University of New Mexico Press.

Kessel, John L. 1987. *Kiva, Cross, and Crown: The Pecos Indians and New Mexico, 1540–1840*. Albuquerque: University of New Mexico Press.

King, Charles S. 2015. "Revolt 1680/2180: Virgil Ortiz." In *Revolt 1680/2180: Virgil Ortiz*, edited by John P. Lukavic, 5–27. Denver: Denver Art Museum.

———. 2021. *Virgil Ortiz*. Santa Fe: Museum of New Mexico Press.

LaMarr, Jean. 1992. *The Submuloc Show / Columbus Wohs: A Visual Commentary on the Columbus Quincentennial from the Perspective of America's First People*, curated by Jaune Quick-to-See Smith, 42–43. Phoenix, AZ: ATLATL.

Last, T. S. 2018. "Board Revises Santa Fe Fiesta Court School Visiting Policy." *Albuquerque Journal*, August 8.

Lippard. Lucy R. 1992. *The Submuloc Show / Columbus Wohs: A Visual Commentary on the Columbus Quincentennial from the Perspective of America's First People*, curated by Jaune Quick-to-See Smith, 9. Phoenix, AZ: ATLATL.

McMaster, Gerald, and Lee-Ann Martin, eds. 1992. *Indigena, Contemporary Native Perspectives in Canadian Art*. Canadian Museum of Civilization: Gatineau, Quebec.

Ortiz, Simon J. 1999. "First Nations, First Peoples, First Voices for Hope and Continuance." *Native, Roots + Rhythms, Journal of the Center for Indigenous Arts & Cultures First Nations, First Peoples: First Voices* 1, no. 1: 1.

Sando, Joe S. 1992. *Pueblo Nations, Eight Centuries of Pueblo Indian History*. Santa Fe: Clear Light Publishers.

———. 1998. *Pueblo Profiles: Cultural Identities through Centuries of Change*. Santa Fe: Clear Light Publishers.

Scofield, John. 1975. "Christopher Columbus, The Sailor Who Gave Us the New World, First Voyage: Westward to Sipangui." *National Geographic Magazine* 148, no. 5 (November): 584–625.

Solomon, Floyd. N.D. Artist Statement.

———. N.D. "Biographical Information," undated document with Artist Statement.

———. N.D. Commentary in Sketchbook, written when Solomon was forty-nine.

———. N.D. Curriculum Vitae.

———. 1992a. *The Submuloc Show / Columbus Wohs: A Visual Commentary on the Columbus Quincentennial from the Perspective of America's First People*, curated by Jaune Quick-to-See Smith, 58–59. Phoenix, AZ: ATLATL.

———. 1992b. Transcript of Interview by Nancy Marie Mithlo, August 22.

———. 1995. Statement for the Wheelwright Museum of the American Indian. Santa Fe, NM.

———. 1996. "Journey to Transcendence." In *Earth, Wind and Fire: Harry Fonseca*, 31–36. Santa Fe, NM: Wheelwright Museum of the American Indian.

———. 1998. "Q & A: From NM to NY." Conversation between Floyd Solomon and Joanna Osburn Bigfeather, conducted by Floyd Solomon. *Indian Market Magazine*.

Vizenor, Gerald. 1999. *Manifest Manners: Narratives on Postindian Survivance*. Lincoln: University of Nebraska Press.

Wilcox, Michael V. 2009. *The Pueblo Revolt and the Mythology of Conquest*. Berkeley: University of California Press.

INDEX